Truth Seekers
·SAGA OF THE SOUTHWEST·

AF271345

Myrtle A. Pohle

Pacific Press Publishing Association
Mountain View, California
Oshawa, Ontario

Cover design and illustration:
Ed Guthero

Phoenix skyline photo: Tom Campbell

Copyright © 1983 by
Pacific Press Publishing Association
Printed in United States of America

ISBN 0-8163-0529-3

Acknowledgments

In this story we have endeavored to give an impartial account of the development and growth of the work of the Seventh-day Adventist Church among the Spanish-speaking people of Arizona. This material has been compiled by churches, according to the order of their organization, followed by accounts of some of the individual members and their experiences in finding the joys of serving a God of love.

I am grateful to Pastors Don Houghton and Jim Taylor, who suggested this work be undertaken, and to the people who have given so generously of their time and have shared their life stories.

Mrs. Mercedes Lenz has been particularly helpful in gathering information and reading this manuscript twice. Others who have read and made corrections and given suggestions include Mrs. Olivine Bohner, Elder and Mrs. James Hardin, Mrs. Lucile Arkebauer, Mr. and Mrs. Brian Quig, Mrs. Gary Parfitt, Dr. Beverly Smith, and Dr. Harold Phillips. To my son, Dr. Charles E. von Pohle, who has given assistance and encouragement, and to all of the foregoing and others who have contributed to this history, my deepest gratitude.

Contents

The Flood

Melchisedec Sanchez listened. "What is that I hear?" he asked his brother.

"It sounds like thunder!" Daniel exclaimed as the two brothers rode down the floor of the gully that led them homeward.

"Look!" Melchisedec pointed. "There's a trickle of water under the horses' hooves! It hasn't been raining. There are no—" Melchisedec never finished the sentence.

Daniel suddenly shouted. "A wall of water! Mama, Papa, the kids!" Daniel dug in his spurs. Melchisedec followed, thundering hooves stirring up dust.

Both boys galloped into the yard, jumped from their panting horses, dropped the reins over the hitching post, and burst into the little house. "Hurry! Hurry!" they shouted.

Lorenzo, their father, accustomed to giving all orders, bristled, but before he could remonstrate with the boys for their rash behavior, he too heard a rumble.

"Everybody get to higher ground quick. A flood! A wall of water! It's coming upon us! Hurry!

Daniel snatched up five-year-old Adiel, while Melchisedec grabbed Abel and rushed up the hillside behind their home.

7

Leonides and Ricardo caught Edisa and Floripe by the hands and scrambled up the rocky slope through the chaparral. The parents followed.

"What caused the flood?" Melchisedec gasped when the family was safe on high ground.

"Remember how white with snow the mountains above us were yesterday?" Daniel answered as he struggled for breath. "Now look at them. With this sudden warm spell the snow has melted, and all that water is rushing down upon our ranch."

As they huddled together on the top of the hill, the Sanchez family looked in dismay upon the devastation of their well-planned homestead near Paguate, New Mexico, which they had spent the past two years getting into shape.

Word of the disaster traveled fast from one settlement to another, from one trading post to another, and the bond of brotherhood among pioneers facing the hardships of an unfriendly desert opened a new horizon to the Sanchez family.

One day in early summer, Daniel brought a letter from the post office. He handed it to his father. Lorenzo opened it and read it in silence. Then he tucked it in his pocket and walked outside.

"That letter came from somewhere in Arizona," Daniel whispered to his mother. "I wonder what it said."

Not until the next morning at breakfast did Lorenzo devulge what the letter said. "We're moving to southeastern Arizona immediately," he suddenly announced.

His wife, Juanita, looked across the table at the children, then back to her husband, who sat at the end of the table, the letter in his hands—the letter that had caused so much curiosity among the boys since its arrival the afternoon before.

"We have no one here to help us through the coming winter. There's no use to hope of getting help from our relatives," Father stated.

"That's right. They call us 'heretics' since we became Baptists," Juanita added.

Lorenzo shook the letter in his hand. "Well, I. E. Solomon invites us to move near him and stake out a claim. He says Melchisedec and Daniel can herd his sheep until we get started. Sixty-three is too old to begin life again, but what else can we do?" Lorenzo raised his voice as though asking a question, but he did not expect anyone to express an opinion.

To Lorenzo's surprise Melchisedec asked, "Papa, when do we start? We boys can help you."

In only a few days the family was packed and ready to start on the great adventure in July 1878. Their transportable possessions consisted of a team of work horses and a covered wagon, food, cooking utensils, and a few saddle horses.

Since Melchisedec was the oldest, Lorenzo assigned him the important task of riding on ahead. Daniel was instructed to follow the caravan to keep Indians from slipping up from the rear.

Toward evening of the first day, Melchisedec galloped back to the wagon.

"What's wrong?" the weary travelers asked. "Are the Apaches coming?"

"No. I've found a beautiful campsite with plenty of grass on the bank of a river. Big alamo trees grow there."

"Thank God!" Lorenzo breathed easily again and urged the horses on until they came to the lush green meadow Melchisedec had described.

After supper, the bedrolls, made of ticking filled with wool, were spread out under the stars. But before retiring, Lorenzo read from the Bible by the light of the campfire and talked of the Creator. By the time he finished, Abel and Adiel had already fallen asleep.

During the monotonous days that followed, the trail led southward and westward over windy, sandy desert. Each night found the travelers perhaps thirty or forty miles nearer their journey's end. At last they reached the Gila River Valley and realized they were close to their destination!

At Pueblo Viejo, later called Solomonville, Mr. Solomon welcomed the Sanchez family. He helped Lorenzo select good land across the river to be staked as a claim. Then he sent Melchisedec and Daniel to herd sheep in the nearby hills.

Little Adiel begged to accompany Daniel and Melchisedec up into the hills. Daniel had always been his favorite brother. How he wanted to go along, but Daniel insisted that Adiel wait until later when they got the sheep camp set up.

Kidnapping Escapes

Later, when the sheep camp had been established high above the Gila River, the two older boys decided to allow Adiel to come with them while they herded the sheep. One warm, bright day the boys heard the sound of thundering hoof beats, and suddenly the air was rent with a blood-curdling war whoop.

"What shall we do with Adiel?" Daniel panicked. "Little brother, why did you come with us this week?" he groaned.

Melchisedec picked up the small boy and ran. "Here, jump into this hollow," he ordered.

"I want to go home," wailed the lad.

"Hush, Adiel. You must be brave." Daniel spread a bedroll over him and inverted a big kettle over his head.

"Now, don't you move, and don't you make a sound!" his brother commanded.

In his cramped position, poor little Adiel shuddered with fright, as his brothers galloped away to meet the Apaches. "Suppose they never come back. Suppose the Apaches steal them," he sobbed softly.

After what seemed hours, Adiel heard horses canter into the sheep camp. What a relief! He almost jumped out from under the kettle. But he realized there were too many hoof beats. "The place must be surrounded by Indians," he thought. "What were they going to do?"

Then he heard Daniel's voice. "He's trying to say Apache words," Adiel whispered to himself. "I hear them laugh. They must have made friends."

Soon the boy hidden in the hollow heard the sound of a crackling fire, the clang of the Dutch oven. "They're making hot biscuits for the Indians!" He sniffed the air. "I smell lamb roasting. Doesn't Daniel remember I'm here? And I'm so hungry." But he remained where Melchisedec had placed him.

Much to Adiel's discomfort, the Indians stayed on and on. Finally, despite his cramped position, he fell asleep. It was dark when the brothers lifted the kettle, wakened him, and assured him that the Apaches were gone. The brothers had saved biscuits and roast lamb for Adiel, who ate as if he had been starved.

Early the next morning, Daniel hurried home with Adiel, safely delivered him to their father, and returned to his work of sheepherding.

The following spring, when Melchisedec and Daniel had moved the sheep to the rolling hills near Mount Graham, Adiel coaxed again to go with his brothers. "Please take me with you. I want to see the beautiful flowers you told me about. I will be a good boy, and you can teach me to play the Indian harp while we are watching the sheep."

"I know you will be a good boy, Adiel. But that is not going to save you from being kidnapped by the Indians," Daniel reasoned.

"But—but—you can hide me like you did before." Adiel's pleading won Daniel's heart.

"Have Ricardo lift you up behind my saddle," Daniel said as he smiled at his little brother.

One afternoon, unannounced, the Indians quietly rode into the sheepherder's camp. This time they were accompanied by their squaws. Daniel noticed one stalwart Indian brave kept looking directly at Adiel. Without taking his eyes off the little boy, the Indian strode directly toward him, hands outstretched to grab him. In an instant one of the squaws snatched the child up and held him tightly, all the while giving orders to the braves in the Apache language. One by one the Indians mounted their horses and rode away. Then the squaw who clutched Adiel put him down and without another word got on her horse and rode into the distance.

After that Adiel decided not to beg Daniel to take him to sheep camp. When he was not attending school, he worked in the fields and gardens until he was ten years old. Then he faced a new danger.

A Scalping Foiled

The hoot-hoot of an owl broke the silence of the night on a grassy tableland near Mount Graham. Father Lorenzo, aroused from light slumber, listened for the howl of coyotes or other predators that might prey upon his flock—the sheep that he had accumulated through much sweat and toil. He heard nothing except the sound of the crickets, baby birds crooning under the cozy wings of their mothers, and frogs, that announced "jug-a-rum, here-I-come," as a bass accompaniment to the cadences of the night. Lorenzo sighed and lay back on his bolster. Cold chills suddenly prickled his skin. There beside him stood the shadowy form of an Indian.

The Apache spoke in soft, almost muffled tones, but the strange voice aroused the two boys, Abel and Adiel, who had accompanied their father. The boys sat up and instantly took in the situation. They had learned enough of the Apache language that they were able to translate for their father.

"Papa," Adiel's teeth chattered as he spoke, "this Indian is our friend. He has slipped away from his camp to come here to tell us we are to be massacred at dawn. He urges us to flee for our lives."

As Adiel attempted to express their gratitude to the

stranger, the Indian blended into the shadows and was gone.

For a few moments the three sat in silence. Then Lorenzo, who had never before asked counsel of his children, turned to the boys and asked, "Shall we abandon the sheep and escape for our lives?"

Adiel, now ten years of age and a born leader—so much like his father—objected to leaving the sheep. "Papa," he suggested, "let's go to the Indians and tell them we are in great trouble because we need to take our sheep across the river, but we cannot do it without their help."

"Will you do the talking?" Lorenzo asked, much to Adiel's surprise.

"Sure," Adiel responded without hesitation.

There was no sleep the rest of the night, as the three talked the situation over and over again and laid plans for transporting the sheep.

Just before dawn, Adiel walked boldly into the Indian camp, followed by Lorenzo and Abel. Bravely the lad marched up to the chief, who was apparently ready to go on the warpath.

After respectfully greeting the chief, Adiel and Abel explained their need of help. The chief looked on in amazed silence. Here were the very ones he planned to scalp, but who could refuse this courteous request from a child? Not even an Apache.

A curt order was given, and the Apaches raced to cut down trees and brush. The logs were fastened together to make barges on which to transport the sheep across the river. In a short time Lorenzo, the boys, and their sheep were all on the south side of the Gila River.

No one but the boys noticed the Apache who had saved their lives make a quick salute, before joining his tribesmen on their way back to the Indian camp.

"Abel, I've had enough escapes from Indians. How about you?" Adiel asked.

"I agree," Abel replied. "It's always over sheep. Everybody knows sheep ruin grazing lands. Maybe Papa would get rid of them if we can find a way to bring in more money from the garden."

Please Send Help!

With the passing of time Adiel and Abel became more and more inseparable. Together they shared their goals and their problems as they worked and planned for the future. Frequently they took wagonloads of produce from their garden to be sold in the mining towns of Morenci and Clifton. This helped support their family.

On one occasion, during their return trip from Morenci, the young men stumbled upon a problem. They had been unable to reach home before midnight Saturday. So they camped until Monday morning and spent Sunday reading, sleeping, and discussing Bible topics. In their minds there was no question as to the importance of baptism by immersion. They were staunch Baptists, but because there was no Baptist church where they lived, the family attended the Methodist church. Their father, Lorenzo, had instilled the truth regarding baptism in the minds of all his children. But now Adiel asked the question, "Why do we keep Sunday as a rest day?"

"Because the Bible says so, of course," was Abel's positive reply.

"Listen to me, Abel. We have heard our father read the Bible all our lives. Now we have read it for our-

17

selves, and I can't find anything about keeping Sunday. It always says *Sabado,* and we know *Sabado* is Saturday, the seventh day, not the first.''

"I'd never thought about it," Abel spoke slowly. "Why don't you write to Pastor Serna, who comes every once in a while to preach in our little church? He will know the answer.''

"That's a great idea. I'll do it right now so the letter can be mailed in Solomonville tomorrow. I'll sign your name too." Adiel grinned at his brother. "It will sound more impressive.''

The letter was soon written and sent on its way to Pastor Serna in Tucson.

Spanish Lessons That Backfired

Sometime before Adiel had written to Pastor Serna, Walter Black, a Seventh-day Adventist colporteur from Healdsburg College in California, and Pastor C. D. M. Williams, who had been sent to Tucson to help the student bookman, knocked on Pastor Serna's door.

Although Pastor Serna listened politely and attentively to the colporteur's canvas, he shook his head as they made their appeal to him to purchase the book. "No," he said, "I don't want any of the books. Thank you. I have plenty already."

The next day Walter Black and C. D. M. Williams called again on Pastor Serna. After a greeting, Walter asked, "You speak Spanish, don't you, Mr. Serna?"

"Oh, yes. That is my mother tongue," Serna answered.

"Would you be willing to teach us Spanish? I have been sent to Tucson to sell books to earn a scholarship to go to college, and such a large percentage of the people speak Spanish that I am handicapped with my sales," Walter requested.

"With pleasure," Marcial Serna assured him.

It was agreed that the Bible would be their textbook. The first Spanish lesson began with Genesis 1. By the time they reached the second chapter of Genesis they were disagreeing over the Sabbath. Since there was a difference of opinion as to which day should be observed, Saturday or Sunday, Marcial Serna challenged the young men to a public debate, which Walter Black stated in the affirmative. "Resolved that Saturday is the Sabbath of the New Testament."

That same day the letter from Abel and Adiel reached Pastor Serna, whose certainty of winning the debate accounts for his hasty reply. It said in part, "I am dealing with two book salesmen on this very subject. We are going to have a debate. I will show from the New Testament that the Sabbath has been changed to Sunday in commemoration of the resurrection of our Lord. I am planning to invite the whole town of Tucson. I will rent the largest place available. As soon as I get through with these young men, I will come and teach you the truth about Sunday sacredness."

C. D. M. Williams remarked to his companion that afternoon after setting up a time for the debate, "Now, Walter, let me help you outline your points for the debate."

"Me! You mean I am going to do the talking? Never! That is up to you. You are a pastor; I am just a student colporteur," Walter protested.

After much discussion, it was finally agreed that Walter would do the talking. So with C. D. M.'s help he prepared a carefully outlined presentation of the Sabbath which covered the Bible from Genesis to Revelation.

By the night of the debate, although he felt certain of his subject, Walter whispered to his friend as they entered the auditorium, "I feel like Daniel must have felt when they let him down into the lions' den." But to his amazement, as he sat down a heavenly peace filled his heart. He opened his Bible to Luke 12:12, as C. D. M.

had suggested, and pressed his finger upon the promise, "The Holy Ghost shall teach you in the same hour what ye ought to say."

As Walter arose following the introduction by Marcial Serna, an inaudible voice said to him, "You have too many notes and have planned too many details." And then the high points of his subject appeared clearly before him.

"Friends, fellow citizens, and highly esteemed opponent, Pastor Serna, my purpose tonight is to show that the seventh day of the week is the Sabbath of the New Testament and that it has never been changed.

"First: Please turn with me to Genesis 2:2 and 3 to see that God introduced the Sabbath to planet Earth at the time of creation. He blessed it and sanctified it.

"Second: The Creator God was Jesus, according to Colossians 1:16. 'For by him were all things created, that are in heaven, and that are in earth.' Therefore, Jesus made the Sabbath.

"Third: Jesus Himself kept the Sabbath. Luke 4:16 tells us that 'as his custom was, he went into the synagogue on the sabbath day.'

"Fourth: Jesus expected His followers to be keeping the Sabbath after His ascension. We know by history that Jerusalem was destroyed about the year A.D. 70. Please turn with me to Matthew 24:20, and we will read what Jesus told His disciples. 'Pray ye that your flight [from Jerusalem] be not in the winter, neither on the sabbath day.' "

Up to this point, Marcial Serna had been busily making notes. But after rereading this text to himself, he quietly put down pencil and pad and sat listening as though transfixed.

"Fifth: The apostle Paul kept the Sabbath. Let us read from Acts 13:14 to 16. In Antioch Paul worshiped on the Sabbath, and verse 44 records that he preached the next Sabbath to the Gentiles. Acts 16:13 tells that at Philippi, where there were no Jews or synagogue, Paul went out by the river to worship on the Sabbath day. Now please turn to Acts 18:4 and 11. In Corinth he 'reasoned in the synagogue every sabbath' and continued there a year and six months—seventy-eight Sabbaths.

"Sixth: The last blessing in the Bible is pronounced upon those that do His commandments so that they may have right to the tree of life. And the Sabbath is in the very center of the Ten Commandments.

"There are two places in the New Testament referred to by many as reasons for worshiping on the first day of the week. The first is Acts 20, which states that Paul and the Christian believers met on the first day, but please notice there were many lights in the room. It was evening. In Bible times, the day began with the setting of the sun. Therefore, the first day of the week 'in the evening' was actually Saturday night. This rules out Sunday worship from this text. The other is 1 Corinthians 16:2. Paul is encouraging the Christians to lay aside in their homes on the first day of the week an offering so they would be prepared to give when he could come. I believe you will agree with me that has nothing to do with Sunday sacredness.

"It will be logical for us to ask where the observance of Sunday originated. Allow me to read to you from just one history, a book entitled *The Great Controversy,* published in 1888. 'In the early part of the fourth century the emperor Constantine issued a decree making Sunday a public festival throughout the Roman Empire. The day of the sun was reverenced by his pagan subjects and was honored by Christians.'

"Now the very name of the day, Sunday—venerable

22

day of the sun—reveals its origin. Sunday has come down to us through tradition, not from the Word of God. Will you please open your Bibles to Matthew 15:9 and read the verse in unison, 'But in vain they do worship me, teaching for doctrines the commandments of men.'

"So, dear friends, I ask you to search your Bibles from Genesis to Revelation. You will not find any indication of a change of the Sabbath to Sunday. Jesus in John 14:15 stated, 'If ye love me, keep my commandments.' Do we love our Saviour enough to follow His footsteps all the way into the kingdom of heaven?"

Walter sat down. There was a breathless silence. Then with all eyes focused upon him, Pastor Serna stood for the rebuttal. But to the astonishment of all present, he announced, "I came here to prove that Sunday is the Sabbath of the New Testament, but these young men have shown me that Saturday is God's Sabbath and it has never been changed. Therefore, from this time forward I will keep the seventh-day Sabbath holy."

Now that the debate was over, Pastor Serna confided to the two new friends his promise made to the Sanchez boys to prove Sunday the Sabbath of the New Testament. "What shall I do?" he asked. "Can you help me?"

"We'll be only too glad to go with you. When do we start?" C. M. D. Williams asked.

"As soon as possible," Pastor Serna replied.

A few days later, the arrangements having been made, instead of going alone, Pastor Serna and his two new friends made the journey together.

How would the Bible Sabbath be received in the settlement of Sanchez? each wondered.

Obedience or Death

"Abel, I can't understand why the young men with whom Pastor Serna debated are coming with him," Adiel remarked as he read the letter from the pastor. "Do you suppose he convinced them that Sunday is truly the Sabbath from the Bible? No matter what they say, I have decided for myself to keep the Bible Sabbath, unless they can give us proof that I have not been able to find for myself," he added.

In Tucson Pastor Serna and his two friends took the Southern Pacific train to Bowie, then changed to a train with destination Globe. After a short ride, Solomonville was announced, and the three found Abel and Adiel waiting at the station. The travelers were taken by horse and wagon across the river to the settlement of the Sanchez family.

During the seven-mile ride Adiel and Abel could not resist asking the all-important question regarding which day is the Sabbath of the Bible. And Pastor Serna tactfully replied, "That is a good question you boys have asked, Abel. It will be answered tonight from the Bible. That and other interesting subjects will be presented by these two young men. They know the Bible from Genesis to Revelation."

That memorable Wednesday evening in the summer

of 1899, the little adobe building that doubled as church and school filled quickly with people anxious to hear Pastor Serna and the young preachers-to-be.

The first meeting aroused so much interest that week after week the Sanchez family and many neighbors continued to listen to the thrilling Bible truths presented. The little meetinghouse where they met had been lovingly built and dedicated. There had been weddings, christenings, and funerals, besides day school, where the grandchildren of Lorenzo and Juanita Sanchez were learning the basics of education. But now events of even greater import were to cling to this little monument which involved decisions that would reach into eternity.

The people listened in rapt attention as the Bible Sabbath was traced, just as Pastor Serna had said, like a thread of gold from Genesis to Revelation.

When the lesson on Bible baptism was presented and a call for those to come forward who would follow Jesus to be buried under the water as He had been, someone exclaimed, "Baptized! We were baptized when we were infants."

Silence filled the room; a foot shuffled; someone cleared his throat. Heads nodded, some in approval, some in disapproval. Then led by Pastor Marcial Serna, twenty-eight slowly arose and walked to the altar. Reverently they bowed, expressing their desire to partake in type the death, burial, and resurrection of Jesus.

The response was so far beyond the expectation of the two young men that they were totally unprepared for this moment of triumph for the gospel.

At the close of the meetings, Walter and C. D. M. talked over the events of the evening.

"What shall we do?" Walter queried.

"Let's contact the headquarters of the Arizona Mission in Phoenix and ask what they advise," C. D. M. suggested."

A letter soon was on its way. When it arrived at its destination, the superintendent was away; so Elder R. M. Kilgore, who was in charge of district number five of the General Conference of the Seventh-day Adventist Church, was sent to Solomonville. Since Elder Kilgore was in Colorado at the time, he traveled directly to the designated town.

When he reached his destination, Elder Kilgore reviewed the great truths of the Bible with the new Sabbath keepers. Early in December 1899, twenty-eight persons were baptized, including Marcial Serna. Then Elder Kilgore organized a church at the Sanchez settlement, the first Spanish-speaking church in Arizona, December 1899.

Lorenzo Sanchez, however, did not become a member of the newly organized church. He had reared his family as an ancient patriarch, to the extent that when he decided it was time for Adiel to be married, he had selected a bride and arranged for the wedding with the parents of Reyes Colvin, an Irish Catholic girl. The young people had never seen each other before they were married. Following the wedding ceremony in the office of the justice of the peace in Solomonville, Reyes was taken to the Sanchez home by her new mother-in-law and father-in-law by horse and carriage. Adiel did not reach home until the following day, because he was required to bring a wagonload of supplies.

Several years had elapsed since Adiel's wedding, but Lorenzo still dominated the lives of his children. Consequently, as soon as the church had been organized, he became greatly agitated when a number of his children became Sabbath-keeping Christians. Urged on in his opposition by former associates who opposed the new teachings, Lorenzo called his family together. With him were the leaders of the agitation and some of his sons who sympathized with them. Realizing the seriousness of the situation, along with the great respect the children held for their father, the new believers felt incapable of facing this crisis alone, particularly when it meant differing with their father for the first time in their lives. Therefore, the new Sabbath keepers asked the Adventist teachers to accompany them in order to buoy up their strength and courage.

In the presence of all, Lorenzo told them they were to give up their new ideas and return to the old faith immediately. "If you do not obey me," he declared, "I will kill every one of you!"

The meeting with Lorenzo ended. There had been no prayer, no reference to what might be God's will. So those who had been threatened asked each other, "Do we follow God, or do we choose our father's way?"

"Reyes, what do you want to do?" Adiel asked his wife. "I am going to keep God's Sabbath regardless of what my father says."

"I will follow you, Adiel, even though we have to sleep out in the bushes," she assured him.

As soon as Lorenzo learned of the decision of Adiel and Reyes, he decided it was time to use force. He drove the young people out of the house, together with their little boy and baby girl. There was no shelter for them except the mesquite bushes and the tarpaulins used at sheep camp.

The next Sabbath afternoon a meeting had been announced for three o'clock. That meeting would decide the final results of Lorenzo's threats. One by one, as three o'clock arrived, all who had been baptized, together with their little ones, made their way quietly and prayerfully into the little adobe church, willing to face death, if that were required of them.

At his home, only a short distance from the little meetinghouse, Lorenzo counted each one who entered the place of worship. He would not allow one to escape.

Solemn was the gathering that Sabbath afternoon. "Will God, who delivered the Hebrew children from the fiery furnace and Daniel from the lions' den, intervene?" The word passed from one to another. Shortly before time for the meeting to close, a messenger rushed to the door of the little church and shouted, "Sanchez boys, your father is dying! He is having a heart attack!"

Chaos reigned as sons and daughters of Lorenzo raced to his side. Adiel gave hasty directions for hitching the fastest team of horses and rushing their father to the hospital in Safford.

His gun, which he had planned to use on those who came out of the meetinghouse, lay unused at home, while doctors labored to save his life. The family paced the hospital corridor, anxiously waiting for word as to his condition. When Lorenzo saw the tender concern of his children whom he had so bitterly reproached—the very ones he had vowed to kill—his heart melted.

"Bring my family to me at once," he gasped.

Cautiously the family entered, not wanting to agitate him with a repeat performance of the previous reunion. Instead, Lorenzo whispered, "Come close, my family." Then beginning with the oldest, he named the children one by one and pronounced a blessing upon each. His words to Adiel, the youngest, were a great surprise to all. "You have been a kind and obedient son. Your father has been pleased with your ways. Now recently you have determined to follow the God of heaven according to your conscience. May God give you the courage and strength to do so.'' There was a pause. Then leaving the care of their mother—his greatest treasure, as he called her—to his children, Lorenzo fell asleep, having given his heart to His Redeemer.

The last traumatic hours of Lorenzo's life served to strengthen the faith and unite those who had begun a new way of life. Each determined to follow God completely, and by their lives of unselfish service to their fellowmen, represent the Saviour. That dedication of more than three-quarters of a century ago is still seen in the lives of children, grandchildren, and great-grandchildren of those who pioneered the work of the Seventh-day Adventist Church in Arizona.

Adiel and Reyes moved back to the parents' home and cared for Juanita until their increasing family necessitated a larger dwelling. The house which Adiel built became a monument of hospitality and treasured memories to guests, children, and grandchildren.

The Sabbath, which had meant so much to the family, remained a precious heritage. As the children and grandchildren grew, they formed a happy chorus around the little organ on Sabbath afternoons, and the big farmhouse rang with songs. Lydia, Adiel's daughter, was official organist by the time she had had her fourth birthday. No, she was not a prodigy. She was born on February 29, so had birthdays only every four years.

Today the precious little organ is treasured in the historical museum of Thatcher, Arizona.

The little adobe church that had been constructed in 1896 when all the family were Sunday keepers was now used for meetings both on Sabbaths and Sundays. It was natural that discussion should arise as to the ownership of the building. So Adiel tactfully called a council meeting. He had, by now, become the accepted patriarch of the clan and mayor of the settlement, honored and respected for his capable leadership and loyal service to God and the community.

During the meeting Adiel said very little as he listened to a long discussion regarding the ownership of the church. Then he quietly remarked, "Well, my brothers, I see we are not going to resolve this problem without someone's willingness to compromise. So you may have the church. I give it to you, and I will build another. However, the land on which it stands is my property. So you may move the church anywhere you want."

Adiel's apparent generosity suddenly changed the whole picture. Eyes grew wide with wonder. One brother looked at another. Nobody had thought how foolish their arguments were. Who would take down an old, weatherworn adobe building and try to rebuild it? So the circumstances settled the question.

The church remained as Adventist property and was used also for the public school, with Adiel and two of his brothers forming the school board. Seventh-day Adventist teachers were hired, and the children of the little community received a good education in the three R's.

The Building Came Too

"What shall we do about our pastor?" the members of the Tucson Methodist Church asked each other the Sunday morning after the debate with Walter Black and C. D. M. Williams regarding the Sabbath of the New Testament.

"Remember what Pastor Serna said after the debate?" someone asked.

"What debate? That didn't turn out to be a debate at all," the head deacon sneered. "Don't you remember what happened? He allowed that young college boy to do all the talking and then agreed with him. I wonder whether he really meant what he said that night. Oh, well, this is the Sunday Pastor Serna is supposed to be in Solomonville. So we won't need to make any decisions until next week."

The following Sunday morning Marcial Serna, without knowledge of the feelings of his church board, hastened down the street toward the little Methodist church. He carried his Bible in his hand and had a new assurance in his step. As he walked toward the little church, he told himself again and again, "I found so much truth I did not know existed. How could I have missed it for so long? Now I must share it with my people here."

As he neared the little church he and his flock had built with their own hands, Marcial Serna's members greeted him warmly. They loved their pastor, the one who had so patiently guided them away from the fears and superstitions that had gripped their lives. He had led them to look in faith to Jesus as the One who had not only paid the full price for their salvation, but also offers the power to live a life of victory and to at last inherit life eternal. How they loved to hear him repeat, "If we walk in the light, as he is in the light, we have fellowship one with another, and the blood of Jesus Christ his Son cleanseth us from all sin." 1 John 1:7. Through his guidance, the members had come to look to Pastor Serna as their spiritual father. So all eyes turned lovingly toward their pastor, as he opened his Bible, ready to present the message.

" 'This is life eternal, that they might know thee the only true God, and Jesus Christ, whom thou hast sent.' " John 17:3. After reading the text, Marcial smiled upon his flock as he began, "My dear children in the Lord, I have recently seen a new picture of my heavenly Father and of Jesus, His Son. I have had a foretaste of life eternal." Then he launched into a beautiful word picture of the work of the Holy Spirit in the lives of the children of God, an experience that God longs to give to each one more than earthly fathers want to give good gifts to their children. "O taste with me and 'see that the Lord is good!' " he exclaimed in closing. Then he added, "And now, dear members, there is so much more to tell you, I don't know where to begin."

"Let's come back here as soon as we have eaten," Atanacio Sarato, the first elder, spoke up.

"That's a good idea." All but one agreed.

During the afternoon Marcial Serna presented the

beautiful lesson of baptism as taught in the Scriptures.

"How did we read these verses for so long and not see what real baptism means? Peter said, 'Repent, and be baptized every one of you in the name of Jesus Christ.' Acts 2:38. What does a baby have to repent of when we sprinkle it?" Several heads nodded approval.

"When Jesus was baptized, Matthew tells us in chapter 3 that Jesus 'went up straightway out of the water.' And you know well the story in Acts 8 regarding Philip and the Ethiopian eunuch. Had you noticed that it says they 'went down both into the water'?

"In closing let's read together Romans 6:4," Marcial Serna suggested. " 'We are buried with him by baptism into death: that like as Christ was raised up from the dead by the glory of the Father, even so we also should walk in newness of life.' "

One day shortly after Marcial Serna's return from the Sanchez settlement, as he taught his flock in Tucson, Atanacio Sarato, one of the members exclaimed, "How beautiful. Now we see why you were baptized in the Gila River. When can we also take part in this wonderful service? Can't the same pastor come here and baptize us?"

"Pastor Kilgore is at the Sanchez settlement now but will gladly come here for a baptism, but first I must teach you many more wonderful things," Pastor Serna replied with enthusiasm.

"Let's meet every night this week," urged Atanacio.

By the time Elder Kilgore had completed his work at Sanchez, Serna proudly took him to Tucson and introduced the members of his little congregation. All the members of that Methodist church but one had accepted the doctrines of the Bible as taught by the Seventh-day Adventist Church. Elder Kilgore studied and

33

reviewed the gospel with these seekers for truth, and on December 31, 1899, he organized the church, in a tent in the old Pueblo of Tucson. In the afternoon they adjourned to a nearby Baptist church, where twenty-three were baptized. That New Year's Eve they met in the home of C. D. M. Williams to complete the work of organization and to appoint officers.

Fifty-one baptized and two churches organized in Arizona during the month of December 1899—the Sanchez church and the Tucson church.

Within a short time the little organization in Tucson made this suggestion: "This building in which we meet actually belongs to us. Why don't we deed it over to the Seventh-day Adventist Church?"

After much thoughtful consideration and counsel, the proper legal proceedings were completed, and the former Methodist-Episcopal church building of Tucson was deeded to the Seventh-day Adventist denomination.

Pima County Courthouse records were completed on February 19, 1901, with the names of Marcial Serna and Atanacio Sarato appearing on the deed.

It seems miraculous that the first two groups of Spanish-speaking, Seventh-day Adventist Christians in the state of Arizona, in the providence of God, had church homes waiting for them at the time of their organization.

A Modern Apostle

"Brother Serna." Elder Kilgore spoke as they were having breakfast together one morning. "The more I am with you, the greater is my curiosity as to how you met the Lord. Do you mind telling me about it?"

"Oh, no, Brother, I am happy to tell you," Marcial Serna replied. "My parents were devout Catholics and reared me with one goal in life—that I should dedicate my life to the priesthood. Consequently it was the objective toward which I worked, feeling certain that as soon as I entered the seminary I would begin a new sphere of my life. Soon I would become sinless, capable of forgiving the sins of others. Then came three distressing years. The more penance I did and the more I struggled to please God, the greater became the burden in my heart. God seemed so far away. At night I would go to the window, and look up at the stars and whisper, 'God, where are You? How can I earn Your love?"

"Why did you say three years? Wasn't the training four years long?" Elder Kilgore asked.

"Yes, but something happened during my fourth year that changed the whole course of my life. I met some Methodist people who introduced me to the study of the Bible and to a God of love with whom I could talk as to a friend.

"Just before graduation I gave up my studies and found work with the railroad in El Paso, Texas, as a telegraph operator. But I had had a taste of the Word of God, and so I devoted every possible moment to reading and rereading the precious Book of books.

"The more deeply I came to appreciate the Saviour and His sacrifice for me, the more I shared this experience with others. My life was filled with the songs of heaven. I wanted everyone to know the good news.

"Soon the Methodist people ordained me to work among the Spanish-speaking people of the Southwest. And that is where Walter Black and C. D. M. Williams found me," he concluded.

"But, Brother Serna, have you considered what this new step you have recently taken will cost you? You have begun to keep the Bible Sabbath. This will automatically cut you off from the support of the Methodist Church. If you receive no salary, how can you keep on traveling from place to place, assuring the Spanish-speaking people that they have been redeemed by the blood of Jesus?" Elder Kilgore asked in perplexity.

"Well, Brother," Marcial Serna spoke slowly and very thoughtfully, "with the apostle Paul I must say, 'Woe unto me, if I preach not the gospel.' I began systematically saving from the time I started working for the railroad and continued after I entered the ministry. I will live on my savings and depend upon the Lord to provide."

Not long after this conversation Marcial Serna was ordained to the ministry for the Seventh-day Adventist Church and became an apostle to the Spanish-speaking people of the Southwest. His ministry was similar to that of the apostle Paul, his ideal. He traveled from place to place, spreading the gospel until the time of his death in 1935.

The Forbidden Book
Still Lives!

In his travels from place to place, Marcial Serna came to the mining town of Ray, more than a hundred miles north of Tucson, where he met both the Carrillo and the Luna families.

"Oh, Brother," Catalina Luna exclaimed, "we have recently come from Mexico. There I had longed with all my heart to read the Bible, and finally a neighbor loaned me hers. But that is a sad story."

"Tell me about it," persuaded Pastor Serna.

Catalina loved to retell the wonderful story. "As I sat huddled over the precious Book the neighbor had loaned me," she began, "I turned the pages nervously and read as fast as I could. I trembled at the sound of any footsteps.

" 'Why should I suffer so much fear?' I asked myself. 'This is God's book—the Holy Bible. That very day I had found a verse that says anyone who meditates on the law of God is blessed and whatsoever he does will prosper. But year after year we live in poverty because we are denied this Book filled with hope of a better way of life. Why must I feel as guilty as a thief, just because someone forbids me to read it?'

"Just as I was asking myself that question, little Carmen entered the room and spoke in subdued tones.

'Little Mother, that new priest, the big man who goes from house to house hunting Bibles and burning them, just came to our block.'

"Pastor, can you imagine how I felt with a borrowed Bible in my home? Hurriedly I wrapped the precious Book in a white cloth, together with a dozen tortillas, and set the package on my head. I hurried down the street to the home of my friend who had loaned me the Bible and quickly gave it back to her.

" 'Did you enjoy the Book?' my friend asked me.

" 'Oh yes!' I told her.

" 'Then why did you not keep it longer?'

"With tears streaming down my face, I told her, 'My little Carmen saw the priest come to our block and enter a home, as he has been doing in other parts of the village. How can the Holy Bible be a forbidden book?' I asked. 'Somehow I feel it is not right. Why are we denied the Word of God here in San Pablo? Is it the same everywhere in Mexico? My heart is hungry to know more, but what can we do? I feel trapped in a hopeless maze.'

"To relieve my pent-up feelings I turned and slowly walked toward the post office. As I strolled among the folk in the marketplace, sitting beside the produce they had spread out for sale, I saw the dear people through different eyes than ever before. I observed the gentle sweetness of the women, weary from hard labor in the fields, many of them with babies on their backs. In their faces I read the same hunger I knew—hunger for love, for peace of soul. 'It is in the Book' I wanted to shout to them.

"You know, Pastor Serna, that the autumn of 1910 General Madero openly called for the people of Mexico to organize immediately in order to overthrow General Porfirio Díaz. There was so much unrest. The people hoped for better times. You can understand why I wanted to tell the dear peasant people that the answer is not in politics, but in the Book.

"Then as a direct answer to my own heart cries, I received a letter at the post office that very morning from my sister, Altagracia Carrillo, with whom we are now living. With joy I read the letter to my husband, Luciano, and our seven children. Altagracia stated in the letter that she and her husband, George, were coming to get us and take us to live with them in the United States. But as we saw the unrest in Mexico ripen into a revolution, we asked ourselves again and again, 'Will Altagracia and George actually come for us?'

"Unspoken thoughts troubled me. I had read in the borrowed Bible that Jesus had promised to come again. So far He had not come. How long must we wait?

"The next day Luciano announced to the children, 'Aunt Altagracia and Uncle George will soon be coming for us. There will be very little room to take anything with us, as they will be coming in a wagon. You must find homes for your pets, so you had better be thinking about that right away.'

"After the last animal had just been disposed of one afternoon the children rushed into the house, each trying to outtalk the other. 'Mama, Papa, come see! There is a wagon with a big round tent on top coming toward the house. Do you think it can be Aunt Altagracia and Uncle George?'

"Our dreams had come true. It was Altagracia and George at last. We were actually going to live in Arizona.

"After supper Luciano and the children went outside with my brother-in-law, George, to examine the wonderful tent on wheels, which George explained is called a covered wagon. While they were all outside, Altagracia started to speak and then stopped. I realized she did not know how to continue. Finally she said, 'Catalina, I am no longer a Catholic.' She then paused and looked at me as though she feared what I might say.

" 'My sister!' I actually dropped a plate and threw my arms around her. 'Do you read the Bible? Can I own one without having to hide it when we live in Arizona?' Then I told her about the borrowed Bible.

" 'That is the first thing I will give you when we reach our home in Ray, Arizona,' Altagracia promised.

"And here is the Bible," Catalina exclaimed, holding it up triumphantly. "Now God has sent you to help us understand it better."

"How long have you had the Bible?" Marcial asked.

"We crossed the United States border on November 22, 1910, and ten days later I had this beautiful new Bible."

Marcial Serna remained a month teaching them. At the end of that time Altagracia Carrillo and Angelita Luna, Catalina's daughter, were taken to Phoenix to be baptized by Elder Serna.

The Sabbath became a day of great joy to the two families. Luciano Luna, a farmer at heart, soon moved his family to Kelvin on the Gila River. Each Friday, however, they packed food and walked the five miles to Ray to spend the Sabbath with Altagracia and her family.

Carmen Luna, a gentle, quiet girl, also asked to be baptized as her aunt Altagracia and her sister Angelita had been. So in 1912, when she was twelve years of age, Elder Serna took the families to the Gila River and baptized Carmen.

Four years later Carmen met and fell in love with

José Romero, a miner. Although José was not of her faith, Carmen married him. Hers was a love that endured for sixty-two years—years full of earnest prayers, as she pleaded for her companion, who never became an Adventist but instead gradually became an alcoholic.

When their firstborn was laid in Carmen's arms, she determined to rear the little girl to be a happy, useful Christian. Eleven more children enriched the home, and each time a new baby arrived, Carmen poured her heart out in loving affection. When Pastor Serna no longer came and she lost contact with Sabbath-keeping Christians, Carmen sent her children to the nearest Protestant Sunday School so they would be taught the Bible. She has lived to see her children develop into noble people, a credit to herself and to the community in which they live.

There were many times when Carmen experienced stormy days and nights of heartache. At fourteen, one of her sons ran away from home with a friend, having decided that life would be easier working in the fields rather than attending school. Carmen took this burden to the One who had become her dearest Counselor. Shortly after, Walter returned home—a much wiser young man.

At seventeen Walter joined the armed forces, and following boot camp, was sent to Korea. These were sad days for American parents who dreaded the approach of a Western Union telegraph messenger, which was the way the government notified families of casualties. Day after day Carmen whispered to God about her boy as she cared for her family. One day she decided to send Walter the best guarantee of his safe return that she could find. Painstakingly she copied the ninety-first psalm, urging her boy to read it often. As

Walter read the carefully penned words, "He shall give his angels charge over thee," the promise became very real to him. In answer to his mother's prayers, one happy day he returned home.

Sometime later he brought home Teresita and introduced her to his mother. "I want you to meet my wife," he said. "We were married last night in Florence."

Four grandchildren finally brightened not only Carmen's life, but that of the children's parents, Walter and Teresina.

Carmen's cup of joy soon overflowed with a new happiness. Walter and Teresina dedicated themselves fully to serve God and keep His commandments. As they counseled with Pastors Don Houghton and Jim Taylor, Walter told them of his mother, who had been so long out of contact with the Seventh-day Adventist Church, but not from her Saviour. The pastors visited Carmen immediately, and she soon had her membership renewed with the church family. From that visit came the inspiration for this book.

The Preacher Who Could Stop a Train

Burt Bray pioneered the work in the territory of New Mexico under circumstances that would shatter the enthusiasm of any but the bravest hearts. The railroad was his main means of transportation. Railroad conductors soon came to appreciate the itinerant preacher's devotion to duty, and would stop anywhere for him.

"Where to today?" the conductor would inquire as Burt boarded a train. "Couldn't your church give you an easier job?"

"Of course," Burt would reply, "but I love my work. And since they gave me this territory, I'm going to do my best." Then he'd find a seat on the train and open his Spanish Bible and a grammar book which he always carried with him. He would study until the train slowed for his destination point.

One other thing, besides his Bible and grammar book, he always carried a lantern. Often the railroad men asked him why he carried it with him.

"Well, you see—" and he paused as if wondering whether he should tell his reason for carrying the lantern. "You see, the bedbugs won't come out as long as I keep the lantern burning."

One day as a conductor helped him onto the train he

inquired, "Man, why did you choose this difficult life?"

"The Lord of glory would have left heaven to save just *one* soul. Can I do less?" Burt Bray had preached a sermon without a text. His life spoke to the frontier railroad men, who ever after looked for the young preacher and always stopped the train wherever he asked to be allowed to get off.

By 1924, Burt Bray, now ordained to the ministry, had been made a part of the working staff of the Arizona Conference for the Spanish-speaking residents. His assignments had taken him to Flagstaff, Globe, and Miami. In 1929 the conference sent him to Tucson to encourage and build up the church members there. With his rich experience in the Spanish work, Burt, along with his two helpers, Antonio Fernandez and José Salizar, put new life into the little church that had almost died. After an evangelistic effort, he reorganized the group with twenty-three members—the same number as the original membership in 1899.

In 1933 Elder W. A. Lusk came to Tucson to pastor the church. The members at that time met in a little adobe building with a dirt floor, which belonged to J. M. Estrada. Elder Lusk began immediately to plan for a new church building. They located a building site at 1101 South Fifth Avenue. The English church group had been holding $800 of the amount for which their former church had been sold, and when this new building project started, they turned it over to the Spanish-speaking group to help finance the new project.

Like a Mother Hen!

As Francis Games came in from a busy morning visiting and praying with members of the Tucson Spanish church, his wife greeted him, "Honey, it seemed you would never get home for lunch today!"

"Why the hurry, Arlene? I have been about my Father's business," was the young pastor's reply.

"Oh, I failed to tell you. There is a letter from the Arizona Conference office in Phoenix. It is not time for our check. What can it mean?" There was a hint of anxiety in Arlene's voice.

Francis took the envelope and opened it. As he read the letter he said, "Arlene, sit down and listen to this."

"What is the matter? You look frightened. Have you been fired?" Arlene spoke rapidly.

"No. Sit down and listen. Elder Atkin is asking us to take charge of the Spanish work for the entire state of Arizona. What shall we do?" Francis groaned.

"Well, I guess they must feel you can do it, or they would not ask you."

"I feel like a mother hen that has been given a whole brooder full of chicks. How can I care for so many dear people? And the first thing Elder Atkin asks us to do is move to Phoenix. What do you think?" Francis waited for Arlene's reply.

"That's simple, Dear. We'll move."

"What would a man do without a good and willing wife? Do you realize it means I will have to travel quite a bit, as there are churches I must visit in Phoenix, Nogales, and Sanchez, as well as scattered members here and there throughout the state?"

"And you did not mention the one nearest and dearest to our hearts at the moment," Arlene reminded him.

"Oh, yes, Tucson, of course." Then after a pause, Francis added, "I am glad Elder Atkin is our president. He is so kind and understanding. We will have many problems, but he and God will help us work them out."

After the family had settled in Phoenix and Elder Francis Games began to realize the magnitude of his task, he approached Elder Atkin. "The only transportation I have is my feet. How can I possibly cover all the territory I need to visit? What shall I do?"

"Well, I have an old Model A Ford that someone gave me on a debt," Elder Atkin spoke thoughtfully. "I will sell it to you for a very reasonable price. We will deduct a small amount from your salary each month until it is paid for."

The plan suggested by Elder Atkin, being agreeable with Elder Games, meant that Games had to secure a license. But soon he and his family set out on an itinerary in the newly purchased car.

They first visited their first church, the church in Tucson. How good it would be to greet the members, who had become like family to them!

The Games family proceeded from Tucson to Sanchez, the church of which they had heard so much but had not visited before.

When they reached Solomonville, seven miles from Sanchez, Francis stopped at the general store operated by Mario Ochoa, a son-in-law of Adiel Sanchez. Mario was known for his outgoing personality and generosity. After the usual introductions and greetings, Mario cautioned, "Don't dare to cross the river now because it is running high. Besides, in this car it's an utter impossibility to reach Sanchez until the river has gone down."

With the inborn curiosity and fearlessness of youth, Francis and Arlene decided to drive down to the crossing and see for themselves how high the river was.

"Look at that Model T!" Francis exclaimed. "It is going through. Now if it makes it across the river, so can we." When the Model T had reached the north bank of the Gila River safely, Francis decided to drive his Model A through the murky water. But soon water was running through the car. Fortunately their five-month-old baby slept in a basket on the back seat. They were almost in the middle of the river when a tire blew.

"We shouldn't have tried this," Arlene lamented and reached back to pick up the basket with baby in it.

"Well, we can't just sit here," Francis answered quickly.

Arlene opened the car door on her side, but Francis admonished, "Don't step down into the stream; you might be washed away, baby and all."

"Well, look! We are blocking traffic. Those large wagons want to cross, and we're in their way," his wife said.

One of the farmers from the wagon behind them sloshed up to the car. "I guess the best thing to do is to pull you out," the burly man said. "It's a good thing I brought a heavy wagon today and not the buckboard."

When they were safe on dry land on the north side of the river, Francis asked, "How much do I owe you?"

"Oh, maybe a pint of whiskey," the farmer replied with a laugh.

"I don't have whiskey. In fact, I condemn whiskey; but I will give you money for the favor you have done for us."

The stranger accepted a cash gift equal to perhaps a day's wages and drove on, only to become deeply chagrined when he later learned that he had accepted money from the preacher who had come to conduct a week of prayer in the Sanchez church.

Francis, Arlene, and baby were welcomed at the big ranch house Adiel had built. Adiel's children and grandchildren formed a happy group as they ran, skated, and played various games on the wide porch which encircled three sides of the dwelling.

Francis noted with pleasure that even the young people and little children attended the meetings which, of necessity, were in the evening, when the men returned from the fields.

One morning, the young pastor shouted to the boys and girls at play, "Let's go to the river."

In recounting the incident recently, one of the grandchildren said, "We piled into his car and filled it to overflowing, some standing on the running boards. He drove like a teenager, and when we reached the river, he threw us all into the water. And he was the pastor! We all loved him, and when he preached we listened."

Arrest the Preacher!

During the summer of 1942 Francis went to Tucson and pitched a tent preparatory to conducting evangelistic meetings. A few days later he was shocked by a policeman who walked up and announced, "You are under arrest!"

"Well, Friend, what have I done?" Francis asked as handcuffs were clamped on his wrists.

The officer, totally unprepared for the friendly smile Francis gave him, finally managed to stammer, "Well—you—you have pitched a—a tent without permission. Therefore, I must take you to headquarters."

Francis tried to explain, but the officer refused to listen. Then much to the officer's discomfort, he discovered it was after five o'clock and the city offices were closed. For an instant he looked perplexed, but on second thought decided to take Francis directly to the mayor's home, where he presented his complaint against the supposed culprit.

"Whom do you represent?" the mayor asked.

"Sir, my name is Francis Games. I represent the Seventh-day Adventist Conference in Pheonix. I am a district pastor and was sent here to conduct Bible lectures. When I applied for permission to pitch a tent in north Tucson, they sent me to this part of town. So I

49

went to your office in south Tucson, and they told me I could put a tent anywhere I wanted to. So I picked the place where it stands on the corner just beyond the Catholic church. It is convenient, and it is in the Spanish part of town.''

The major gave a withering look to the policeman of Mexican extraction and said, ''You know in this country we cannot interfere with religions. Anybody has the right to preach where he pleases, so leave this man alone.''

Without a word, the officer released Francis and drove quickly away, leaving him to walk back to the tent.

About two weeks after the arrest incident, a man was murdered on that very corner. The people became afraid. But in spite of the trouble, a few people faithfully attended the meetings and were baptized. Among them were members of the Estrada and Rangel families.

The church in Tucson continued to grow. It became crowded and the church members all agreed that they needed a new and larger building. The Sabbath School rooms were not adequate for the children, and a new dining room where they could feed guests on Sabbath was a necessity.

A committee, appointed to search the city of Tucson for a satisfactory location for the new church home, was formed, but there seemed to be no site available for a new and larger building.

At last it was decided to tear down the old building and put up a new one on the same site.

''How many church buildings have we had in Tucson so far?'' one of the newer members asked.

One of the older members replied, ''There have been three—the original church donated by the congregation of Elder Marcial Serna in 1901. Then there was the church on East Ninth Street, dedicated in 1916. In 1938 this building was finished. So our new one"—he began to talk as though it were a reality—"will be the fourth."

"Now, let's plan this building so well that it will still be in use when Jesus comes," several members said.

A beautiful spirit of harmony and zeal existed among the members. Those responsible for the technical construction were Dan Parra, Paul Sanchez, Gilberto Tobar, Gildardo (Ed) Baldenegro, assisted by many of the loyal members, both men and women. And on June 17, 1972, the new church was dedicated free of debt.

Section Three:
The Phoenix Church, 1910

Pioneers for Christ

In 1899 two churches had been established in southern Arizona. But what about the people of Phoenix who spoke the beautiful Spanish language?

God *did* have plans for them which started way back in 1868 when Elders John N. Loughborough and D. T. Bordeau pioneered evangelism in California. The fascinating story of how their evangelism reached Phoenix we gathered from Mrs. Jessie Bond-Johnson, ninety-seven years of age when she related this story.

"Soon after he had been converted in the meetings held by Elders Loughborough and Bordeau in California, my uncle Seth came to visit us," Mrs. Johnson told us. "Day after day he followed my father to the field, talking incessantly of his newfound hope of a soon-coming Saviour and of the Sabbath.

"Mother became so alarmed at Seth's enthusiasm that she remonstrated, 'Seth, we love you and you are welcome to come to our home any time you want to, but don't talk about that Sabbath business. James is a Baptist and I am a Methodist. If you keep on talking and talking about Saturday being the right day to keep you will confuse our children.'

"Uncle Seth tactfully went home, but assured my father of his prayers and left some tracts for him to study. He also asked a Sabbath-keeping neighbor to visit my father.

"One day Mother vehemently exploded, 'James Monroe Bond, do you mean to tell me you have been sneaking out to the barn and reading those pamphlets Seth left?'

" 'Yes,' Father quietly replied, 'and I went to the Adventist church last Sabbath.'

"This shock was too much for Mother, who burst into tears and exclaimed, 'Now our children will grow up atheists!'

" 'Sarah, if you will allow me to study the Bible with you, I can show you that Saturday is the Sabbath of the Bible,' Father coaxed.

" 'You can't do it. I can prove from the Bible that we are supposed to keep Sunday,' she vowed.

" 'All right, Sarah, if you can prove to me that Sunday is the Sabbath, I will keep it with you the rest of my life,' Father promised.

"The entire next Sabbath Sarah and James Bond and Uncle Ebenezer spent in searching the Scriptures from Genesis to Revelation. Father read quotations from the pamphlets Uncle Seth had left which gave the dates and history of Sunday observance being introduced from pagan sun worship into the church more than 300 years after the crucifixion.

"By the close of the day my family was united in their beliefs. Slowly but surely the wonderful Sabbath truth had found its way into Mother's heart, and once she saw it, she faithfully kept the Sabbath the remainder of her life and lived with the assurance of a soon-coming Saviour.

"From the moment that Mother and Father were united in the observance of the Sabbath, they became obsessed with a burning desire to share the good news.

53

Father went to medical school in order to better prepare himself for his new task. Then when finished, he opened an office in Hanford, California.

"Among Father's patients were many Spanish-speaking people to whom he wanted to give the good news of the gospel. Therefore, he hired a bilingual lady to teach us children to become his translators.

"How little did my parents dream of the extent of their work in preparing pioneers for the Spanish work in various parts of the world! Three of my brothers—Frank, Walter, and Ernest—lay down their lives while carrying the gospel to Spanish-speaking people, and Lester went as a missionary to Cuba."

About 1900 Frank, Walter, and Ernest came to Phoenix to earn scholarships by selling religious books to the Spanish-speaking people. Frank had finished college by this time, so we conclude he must have been working to pay off a school indebtedness or to help his younger brothers. In 1902 Walter and Frank volunteered to go to Spain to pioneer mission work in that country.

After a term of service overseas, Walter and Frank returned to Phoenix and held an evangelistic effort, which resulted in the organization of a group of believers—the nucleus of the work for Spanish-speaking people in the Phoenix area. Since there was as yet no place for the Sabbath keepers to meet in Phoenix they met in a tent. But shortly after organizing the small church group in Phoenix, Frank and Walter both returned to Spain to carry on the work begun there. Walter died while on a missionary journey in Spain. Frank, however, continued to work until ill health caused his retirement in 1923.

From Here to There

The Spanish-American Training School opened in 1920, and Sabbath services were conducted in Spanish at the school located on North Fourteenth Street, south of what is now McDowell Road. Teachers from the training school helped pastor the growing church.

By 1921 the members had found land and constructed a house of worship in south Phoenix at 711 South Montezuma Avenue. How the members loved their new church. Eagerly they shared with their relatives and friends their newfound faith, and their beloved house of worship became too small for the growing membership.

"What shall we do about a new building?" members began to ask.

Elder W. H. England helped to find lots at 350 West Mohave, which were approved by the church board and the Arizona Conference. Under the guidance of Pastor Augustine Cortez, and with Elder W. R. French in charge of construction, the new church was built and ready for use in 1954 and dedicated in 1955.

There was no such thing as announcing a work bee and pleading for people to help during the building program. The members eagerly came, and even the women climbed ladders with boards in their arms.

Spanish dinners, supervised by Maria Galindo, were prepared to help raise funds. Young and old alike shared in the joys of working together. The church on Mohave was very much their church. Hadn't they built it with their own hands; hadn't they bought the blocks on the drawing board at fifty dollars each to purchase building supplies?

Through the inspiration and influence of the pastors and members, this beloved church also became too small. The growing congregation felt the need of bigger and better accommodations. Thus it was on a Wednesday evening at prayer meeting that the members suggested, "Let's pray that we can sell this church and build another."

"While we are finding a buyer, there will be plenty of time to purchase a good location and begin to save toward the building fund," the pastor, Elder Saul Visser, agreed.

A dream had been born. Everyone went home, pleased with the decision. However, no one, not even Pastor Visser, was prepared for the sudden change in their plans. As he entered his home following the prayer meeting, the telephone rang. A strange voice asked, "May I speak to Pastor Visser, please?"

"This is he," was the reply.

"Pastor, would you be at all interested in selling your church building?" the stranger asked.

Was he hearing correctly? What should he say? "Lord, we are not ready for You to answer so soon!" The thoughts raced through Elder Visser's mind. "If we sell now, where will we meet for services? Perhaps we should call a church-board meeting and also ask the conference directors before giving an answer." Since God had acted so promptly in answering their prayer, he too would act quickly. So taking the name and telephone number of the calling party, Elder Visser went to work in great haste.

Much to everyone's relief the Arizona Conference leaders approved the sale and suggested, "Why not meet in Fattebert Hall on Fifteenth Street? The conference owns the building, and it is not being used regularly."

Feverishly the members searched for a new site. Then God had just the right man ready to draw the plans and engineer the construction of the new church at 4408 North Thirty-fifth Avenue, the new site. Brother José Schmied gave so much of his expertise and devotion to the new church home that some of the members even affectionately called it "Brother Schmied's Church."

The building committee consisted of Pastor Saul Visser, Engineer José Schmied, Leandro Vega, Jr., Rafael Orduño, Norberto Galindo, Alicia Galindo, and Nellie Hanan. William Stansbury was the builder.

In 1972 the new church home was ready for occupancy and dedicated with great joy two years later. The pews, which add greatly to the comfort of worship, as well as beauty to the sanctuary, were a gift from José Rodrigüez in memory of his mother, Mrs. Refugio Rodrigüez.

The Phoenix church on North Thirty-fifth Avenue is glowing with the joys of the gospel. It can be felt in the very atmosphere as one enters. It was my privilege to worship with the Phoenix Spanish Seventh-day Adventist church members on March 28, 1981. The church family was preparing for a special evangelistic effort to be led by Pastor G. Bustamante.

Now, after the meetings, we have learned twenty-five persons have dedicated themselves to God and have been baptized.

A very unusual part of the program is the devotion of the church members to the aged and shut-in. Sabbath morning members go to their homes and pick them up. The front pews at the church are reserved for them. What precious memories of joys and sorrows, of tears and triumphs, these dear aged ones, who have spent many years walking the pathway heavenward, still treasure.

Perhaps by turning back the pages of time and reviewing a few of the heartwarming stories of the past we shall gain new courage to press forward and finish the work of God on earth and be ready to spend eternity with God's faithful children.

Gospel From the Neighbor's Garbage

When Isabel Vega's husband returned from work one day, Isabel met him at the door. "Leandro! Leandro, listen to me! At last I have found it!" Isabel Vega exclaimed.

"Why all the excitement? What was lost? And where did you find it?" Leandro calmly asked.

"Some girls came today." She paused to catch her breath. "I tell you some girls came today and—"

"What did they want? Anyway, how could you understand them?" Leandro's second question was practical, because Isabel had not yet learned to speak English.

"They were Mexican girls—*Sabatistas!* They have had services on Sabbath at the very place where we attended the camp meeting."

"But—but—there's no church there. That's a school there now." Leandro's enthusiasm began to ebb.

"Yes, I know. The girls said they had had services in Spanish at the school until the new church was built on Montezuma Avenue. When I told the girls I had walked the streets of Phoenix for seven years looking for a church that kept the Bible Sabbath, they gave me a big hug. I thought one of them would cry. They were so happy when they left here and said they would ask

59

the pastor to come see us soon, and we are to go to church next Sabbath with them." Isabel paused for a moment, and then went on. "Leandro, won't it be a thrill to read the Bible and listen to good messages from one of our own faith?"

"Isabel," Leandro replied slowly, "I can't read, you know."

"Oh that won't make any difference. You are a good listener. You probably know as much about the Bible right now as those girls. I have been reading to you for so many years. Just think! Ever since we lived in Cananea and I bought the Bible from the little boy who came to play with Fermin, we have been reading every day. Now I will read even more as we learn new ways of studying God's Word."

Not many days passed until the pastor of the Spanish church, Burt Bray, called on Leandro and Isabel.

"I have come to pray with you and to invite you to attend church on Sabbath morning," Pastor Burt Bray began. "Tell me, how did you become Seventh-day Adventists?" he asked.

"What are Seventh-day Adventists? Is that the name of the church that keeps the Sabbath?" Leandro asked.

Burt Bray seemed unprepared for this question. He paused for a moment and then went on, "Please tell me, where did you learn of the gospel?"

Without any hesitation, Isabel replied, "From the neighbor's garbage."

"From the neighbor's garbage?" Pastor Bray exclaimed. "How could that be?"

"One day while we were living in Cananea, Sonora, Mexico, a little boy came to play with our boys. He carried a Bible in his hand. I asked him what it was. He told me, 'I found this book in the garbage. My mother does not want it in the house.' I bought the book from him for a few cents. I began reading the Bible not only for myself but also to my husband. The Lord was leading us all the time, and we did not know it.

"In 1920 we moved to Phoenix, and Leandro went to work on the ranch of Mr. Tom Sullivan, who was a *Sabatista*. While we were working there Mr. Sullivan invited Leandro and me to attend a camp meeting in a field on North Fourteenth Street. Some of the meetings were in Spanish, and our hungry hearts drank in every word. When the meetings ended, we kept the Sabbath, but could not find a church. As I told the girls, I have walked up and down the streets of Phoenix looking for a place to worship. Now God has answered our prayers."

The following Sabbath, early in June 1929, Leandro, Isabel, and their four boys received a royal welcome at the new church for Spanish-speaking people. By October they were baptized and became happy, active members of the church family. Leandro and Isabel began to share their new joy with others. Whenever a need was presented, they were among the first to respond. The day Leandro was ordained as a deacon he felt his cup of joy was full.

In 1942 Leandro's son, Leandro Junior, graduated from the Arizona Academy, the school which had been built on the very land where Leandro and Isabel had first learned of the Bible Sabbath.

Isabel has been alone now for many years, but at ninety-two still awaits the coming of Jesus. When the Phoenix temperature registered 113° we found her caring for her flowers, her face radiant with the love of the Saviour. She spoke proudly of Leandro Junior. "He is the treasurer of the church and helps the pastor a great deal, just as his father did for many years."

From Hate to Love

The morning breeze caught the piercing scream that came from the house on the southern end of Lake Sayula in Mexico's state of Jalisco. Dolores Quintero heared the scream and started to rush into the house to see what had happened to her little sister, Carmen.

Carmen, with blood streaming down her arm, ran toward her sister. The little girl held her hand tightly over her ear.

"Oh, Carmen, what has that woman we are supposed to call mother done to you now? Let me see." Dolores ushered Carmen into their own room.

When Carmen took her hand from her ear, Dolores, to her horror, saw that the stepmother had grabbed Carmen's ear in such a way that her earring had been torn completely out and with it, a lower portion of her ear.

"Listen to me, Carmen. We have endured enough," Dolores said in a sympathizing voice. "Papa does not believe us when we try to talk to him about our painful existence here with this stepmother. We *must run away*."

"When shall we go? And where could we go?" Carmen whispered between sobs. "I wish our mother were living."

"I have heard that Guadalajara is a big city and that rich people hire young girls to do their housework," Dolores told her sister. "They say the servants live in rooms back of the big houses and have good food. Even if the people do not treat us kindly, it can't be as bad as staying here.

"For a long time I have been planning to run away," Delores continued. "The only thing that has kept me here is my love for you. Now I will take you with me. We will go before dawn, when the women are walking to Atoyac with their produce. Perhaps some of them will feed us. If we stay on the main road that follows the railroad, someone may come along who will give us a ride part way. Somehow we will reach Guadalajara." Dolores planned aloud in soft tones, as she endeavored to wash away the blood and examine the portion of the ear that remained.

As planned, Dolores and Carmen left their home early the next morning. Upon their arrival in Guadalajara they were advised to wait near the market where people often looked for domestic help. In this way, both girls found work in different homes. It did not occur to them that they had failed to find out where the other was going or that they could become permanently separated. But it happened! They never saw each other again.

Carmen worked in first one home and then another, enduring the cruel wrath of the housewives or the abuse of servants of longer standing, who became jealous of her because she did her work well.

Then, one wonderful day in 1900, when Carmen was fifteen years of age, she went to work for an American family who spoke kindly to her and to each other. In the home of Elder and Mrs. James A. Leland, Seventh-day Adventist missionaries, a new life began for the motherless girl. She found the family her heart had longed for.

Four happy years slipped by. Then one day Mama Leland confided to Carmen, "It is time for us to return to the United States. We shall be leaving soon."

"Mama Leland, you won't leave me here, will you?" Carmen pleaded.

That was just the reply Mrs. Leland had hoped for; so arrangements were made to take the girl, who by now was so much a part of the family, with them.

In their new home in Albuquerque, New Mexico, Carmen tenderly cared for the children, nursed them through sickness and health, and wept over the death of one from typhoid fever. Then some years later in 1907, Carmen Quintero married Juan Garcia. The couple had never seen each other until the day of the wedding. Perhaps Elder Leland had arranged the marriage, as was the custom among Spanish-speaking people.

Juan and Carmen went to live first in Tucson and later in Glendale, Arizona. Juan became a Bible instructor and assisted Elder Frank Bond in the evangelistic work in Phoenix.

It is difficult to comprehend what Carmen accomplished in one lifetime. She dedicated herself to midwifery, bore ten children, and adopted an eleventh.

Her daughter, Mrs. Carmen Escudero, told us that when she was growing up no matter what time of day or night it might be, when people knocked at their door to say they needed help, her mother always did what she could to help them. Many times she never received pay for her work. At times she received a chicken or wood for the stove. If a family was destitute, Mother would gather up linens, and go to the store for supplies of food for the needy family.

"Although neither of my parents had any formal

education," Mrs. Escudero continued, "both learned to read and write English and Spanish. My father became a naturalized American citizen on March 26, 1941, and Mother, on April 23, 1942.

"Mother worked very closely with Dr. Philip Rice of Glendale. When she saw a birth was not going to be normal, she would send for him, or even at times he would send for her, because she had a way with the Mexican people. She delivered babies for mothers of all races, single births and twins, as well as most of her own grandchildren. It is estimated that she helped in the delivery of almost half of the Spanish-speaking population of the city of Glendale.

"The lives of my parents had made such an impact on the people of Phoenix and Glendale, that in 1950, when my father passed away at the age of seventy-eight, even the governor of Arizona wrote a letter of condolence to Mother."

The Bone I Could Not Pick

"You know what it is like to step into a brilliantly lighted room after being out on a dark night. At first you are blinded, and that is what would have happened to me," Carlos Ayala said as he reminisced about his conversion. "If I had come face-to-face with all the Bible truths at once, I could not have endured it. Instead, I, who had been born in Mexico City and reared a Catholic, was led gradually to God. I am always amazed when I realize with what loving determination, yet tenderness, He led me.

"My first contact with Protestants was in Tucson, where I went into the bakery business with a Baptist in 1915. He baked the bread and I delivered it.

"In making my sales, I passed the place where Elder Marcial Serna, the Seventh-day Adentist pastor, was holding meetings. In Mexico I had heard that Protestants worshiped a calf, so from curiosity I peered through a small opening into the meeting place. What did I see? Pastor Serna was preaching with charts illustrating the beasts of the seventh chapter of Daniel.

" 'In reality the Protestants do worship a calf,' I assured my partner, 'because I saw pictures of beasts as Pastor Serna preached!'

" 'Oh, no, Carlos. You just don't understand,' he

explained. 'I think he must have been representing the characteristics of nations spoken of in Bible prophecies, using beasts as illustrations. You know they say one picture is worth a thousand words. Haven't you ever read the Bible?' my partner asked me.

" 'No, of course not. I leave that to the clergy.' I tossed that reply over my shoulder as I went to deliver bread. I thought I had given him a good reason.

"The next day my partner talked to me as he helped load the bread. 'Carlos, suppose I am in California and you want to come there, so I write you directions in detail. You leave my letter on the table at home and start driving east toward El Paso, Texas.'

" 'I'd never get there,' I retorted.

" 'No, of course you wouldn't. But that is the way you plan to reach heaven.'

"By that time the bread was loaded, and he walked into the bakery, leaving me to ponder my eternal destiny that I had so irresponsibly left in the hands of someone else.

"In various tactful ways, my partner finally convinced me to read the Bible for myself. In the end he convinced me to become a Baptist. I felt very good about my new concept of God and was pleased to call myself a Protestant. Then I proudly shared the Baptist faith with my mother and my sisters.

"When my mother, my sisters, and I moved to Phoenix, we found no Baptist church, so I began attending the Methodist Church, and in a short time I had become a Sunday School superintendent.

"One Sunday I invited a Sunday School member to my home for dinner. During the meal he told me about a man who worked in the fields with him who was a *Sabatista* and talked a great deal about it to his fellow workers.

"Adolfo, my brother, had read a tract which said the *Sabatistas* cast reflection against Jesus when they keep Sabbath and suggested we send it to the man. The *Sabatista* must have told Brother Juan Garcia, the Bible instructor for the Adventist church in Phoenix, about Adolfo's sending the tract, because he came immediately to see Adolfo.

"The next time I saw Adolfo, my first question was, 'How did it go with you and the *Sabatista?'*

" 'They are right! We are dealing with the law of God.' Adolfo spoke with conviction.

" 'You don't know much,' I blurted out. 'Leave him to me.' I was disgusted with Adolfo's ignorance, so he referred Brother Garcia to me, who began giving me Bible lessons also. Of course, I watched his every move, trying to find some fault with what he was teaching.

"I was an electrician for the shops of the Phoenix streetcar company when Brother Garcia began studying with me. Soon they changed me to a substation at Glendale, where I started the generators early in the morning and turned on the switch. Then the remainder of the day I could do as I pleased. Since God put me where I had much time for study and thought, I told myself, 'Now I will find truth.'

"During the weeks that followed, the Methodist pastor visited me, a Presbyterian pastor found me, and the Baptist pastor came also, as well as a colporteur, and then on Saturday Brother Garcia would come.

" 'Everybody uses the verses that please him,' I said, somewhat confused by it all.

"But one day the Baptist brother said to me, 'I am going to give you one verse. With that you will forget the Seventh-day Adventists. It is Galatians 2:16.

" 'Oh, poor little Brother Garcia!' I exclaimed.

68

'Now I am going to match wits with him.' So the next Sabbath, when Brother Garcia came, I said, 'Brother, I have a bone to pick with you.'

"I read Galatians 2:16 to him.

" 'Read it again,' he said.

"So I did. 'Knowing that a man is not justified by the works of the law, but by the faith of Jesus Christ, even we have believed in Jesus Christ, that we might be justified by the faith of Christ, and not by the works of the law: for by the works of the law shall no flesh be justified.'

"Brother Garcia laughed until he became tired. 'Very well,' he said. 'What do you think this means?'

" 'That we don't have to keep the law of God.'

" 'Oh, no, Brother,' he replied. 'If I say that your shoes are not to be put on your head, does that mean you must go without shoes? No, you must wear your shoes on your feet and not on your head. The verse says *we* are not saved by *our* works, but we are justified by the faith of Jesus Christ, who kept the law and made it possible for us to do the same.' Then he read 1 Corinthians 7:19, 'Circumcision is nothing, and uncircumcision is nothing, but the keeping of the commandments of God.' This explanation made it so clear to me that I became a Seventh-day Adventist Christian, redeemed by the blood of Jesus.

"When the Spanish-American Training School was started in Phoenix in 1920, we had been studying with Brother Garcia for two years. Immediately I was recommended to Elder Henry Brown, the first one in charge of the Spanish department of the school. He came to see me, and his first questions were, 'Do you know the message well? What do you plan to do about keeping the Sabbath?'

"I knew I couldn't work for the streetcar company

69

and keep the Sabbath. 'I am thinking about saving enough money to start a small grocery store,' I replied.

"Elder Brown laughed. 'No, young man, not that! If you find it difficult to keep the Sabbath where you are, you'll find it much more so with a store. What you need to do is get down on your knees and say, "Father, help me to keep the Sabbath, even though I die of hunger." Let me assure you, the Lord will help you.'

"And the Lord did what He had promised. I went to my knees, and then resolved to keep the Sabbath no matter what happened. I decided to ask the superintendent and the director for Sabbath off when I found them together, instead of one at a time.

" 'I cannot work on Saturday anymore,' I told them.

"The superintendent asked, 'Is it a matter of religion?'

" 'Yes, Sir.'

" 'We will think about it,' was his reply.

" 'Very well, but while you are thinking, don't count on me to work on Sabbath.' I was the only electrician at the time, and there was enough work on Sabbaths for twenty. Since I had learned that we do not work for men, I had done my work as though I were in the presence of an all-seeing God, a practice which pleased my superiors. They ignored my request by never saying Yes or No, but I never worked another Sabbath.

"Elder Brown soon had me convinced that I should attend the training school, a decision for which I am very thankful.

"In 1923 the conference sent me as a Bible instructor with Brother Serna to a little town called Homeland in New Mexico. There, with God's help, I raised up a congregation of about twenty. Unfortunately, when we came to the worker's meeting in Phoenix, I became

70

discouraged. The streetcar department of the city offered me work with Sabbaths off, and I listened to the devil and left God's work.

"If I had had the good wife God gave me two years later, I might have remained in the ministry; but it was not until 1923 that Carolina Salazar came to Phoenix to attend the training school, and, as I mentioned, we were married two years later. Carolina's father, Pastor Ybaño Salazar, accepted the message in New Mexico in 1914 through the work of José Maria Lopez, a colporteur.

"It was not until many years later that I would learn some of the results of my work in Homeland. Carlos Junior, our son, went with Elder Games to hold an effort in Barstow. There they found a couple who had been keeping the Sabbath alone with no association with other Sabbath keepers for twenty-five years.

"When this family read the announcement of the meetings that Pastors Carlos Ayala and Francis Games were going to conduct, the husband said, 'Look, Brother Ayala is still preaching!'

The wife assured him, 'That has to be his son.'

"All those years since I had been in Homeland, this couple had been faithful to the message I had taught them.

"God has been good to us. Our girls are all serving the Lord. Carlos Junior is awaiting the call of the Life-giver. He died in the full hope of the soon coming of Jesus. We plan to be a united family in heaven."

Alone! Penniless! Lost

Alone! Penniless! Miles from home in a strange city! How did a sixteen-year-old girl get herself into such a situation?

A year before that fateful day, Sally and her sister, Emma, had cried together. "What shall we do? Crying is not going to help us. We tried living with our mother and stepfather. They don't want us."

The two girls came to Solomonville where their father lived. But here they found they couldn't go to school or attend church. "And," Emma said, "our father does *not* want us; that's plain to see."

"Emma, let's get an education and be somebody. We'll show them. Someday they will be proud of us." Sally spoke with conviction.

"But where can we go, and how can we attend school?" Emma wondered.

"We have lots of relatives in Phoenix. Let's go there. I am going to try Uncle Carlos and Aunt Carolina." Sally began to plan. "Why don't you try Aunt Vicenta? She will take you to church."

A few days later, Sally announced to her aunt and uncle in Phoenix, "Here I am." She dropped her suitcase on her uncle Carlos Ayala's front steps. "I want to go to school and get an education."

Sally found a welcome in her aunt and uncle's home.

Sabbath morning all the family, including Sally, went to church. At the dinner table one Sabbath afternoon, Sally remarked to her cousins, "What a wonderful pastor you have! He is interested in me, as though he had known me all my life. I never met a pastor with so much feeling of love for everyone. I am sure I want *him* to baptize *me*."

Sally enrolled at the Phoenix Central High School and soon impressed her teachers with her outstanding abilities to the extent that they helped her to complete the college entrance requirements the following summer.

At home with her aunt, uncle, and cousins, she announced, "Cousin Carlos is going to Pacific Union College in California. It must be a wonderful school by the way you talk. I have decided that if he goes there, I can too."

Having expressed her secret determination, Sally's plans began to materialize. Relatives began showering her with items she would need for her great adventure. Each new gift she carefully packed in a trunk her mother had given her.

The day of her departure finally arrived. The family helped her take the trunk to the bus station, where she asked for a ticket to Pacific Union College.

"That is too large," the ticket agent growled, pointing to the trunk. "We don't ship trunks by bus. You will have to go by train."

They all hurried to the Southern Pacific station.

"Where to?" the ticket agent asked, as the girl presented herself and the precious trunk at his window.

"To Pacific Union College," Sally proudly replied.

A ticket was issued in exchange for all the money Sally possessed, and she boarded the train, only to be

73

put off with her trunk at Stockton, California.

"Where is Pacific Union College?" she asked the station agent.

"Pacific Union College!" he exclaimed. "It's not around here. The College of the Pacific is here." After some inquiry the station agent said, "You will have to take a bus tomorrow morning to a place north of here called St. Helena, and from there they will take you to the college seven miles farther up on Howell Mountain."

Miles from her destination, she stood beside the trunk—her only worldly possession. Alone and penniless, she made her way to the telegraph office and explained her situation. An understanding telegraph operator said, "We'll wire your family for money for your ticket and enough more to cover this message, so that when it comes you can pay us." God miraculously took a hand in Sally's perplexities and provided a place for her to stay overnight.

Four years later Sally was again traveling. This time with a college diploma, she was on her way to teach in Hawaii. The following summer, she was sent to Montemorelos, Mexico, to become certified to teach Spanish. While there she met one of the instructors, Sam Torres. They were married two years later. Together they taught for three years at Montemorelos, then for nine years in Calexico, before going to La Sierra.

In a short time Sam was laid to rest; but Sally continued teaching and now fills the position of vice-principal of La Sierra Academy. Through the vicissitudes of life Sally has developed a priceless perception and empathy for young people seeking an answer to life's problems.

Gospel in an Outhouse

"O holy Virgin, please implore your Son to have mercy on us. Why is heaven so much against us?" Geronima Fernandez did not intend to complain, but there was an inexpressible unrest and emptiness in her heart that nothing seemed to satisfy. At night, after the little ones were asleep, she often went outside and looked up at the stars while she tried to find an answer. Again and again she asked herself, "Why are we here on this earth? What does the future hold? If we displease the God of heaven, why must we spend an eternity in hell?"

One day Geronima found a portion of a torn-up book in the outhouse. Who put the book where it was, nobody knows. But there in the outhouse Geronima found the torn pages. Carefully she tried to piece them together. She read and reread the portion that she had found and had been able to put together.

When Marciano Hernandez, a regular vendor, drove up to the Fernandez home on Seventh Street, Geronima hurried into the house and brought out the treasured pages of the book, *The Great Controversy*, that she had found.

"Can you get a copy of this book for me?" she asked.

Now strange as it may seem, Marciano Hernandez was a Seventh-day Adventist. The book was familiar to him. He promised that the very next time he came, he would bring the book she wanted. To add to Geronima's joy, Marciano offered to have someone come to teach her and her husband Pablo how to study the Bible.

Soon the Fernandez family was receiving Bible studies, and Marciano Hernandez took them to church in Phoenix each Sabbath.

Pablo, who was in poor health, passed away in May 1932, before his baptism took place. Geronima, however, felt Jesus had been baptized for those who were not able to take part in this blessed rite, and lived in full confidence of meeting him to spend eternity together.

After fifty years, the three living daughters still hold bright the hope of meeting their parents in the earth made new. "When we were little," one of the daughters told me, "we wanted to read the part of the book that had meant so much to our mother. The pages were yellow and brittle, so she guarded them like a treasure. It was something sacred to all of us, because through those pages torn from *The Great Controversy* we had come in contact with the ones who taught us the way of life."

Bible From a City Dump

"It seems unbelievable that hunting for firewood in the Phoenix city dump could have a part in leading anyone to the Lord, but that is the way it was with our family," Nellie Gallardo-Hanan explained.

"We lived on Sixteenth Street and Shea Boulevard. My mother raised chickens and turkeys, and many of them were being run over by passing cars. So when Mother sent my brother Perfecto and sister-in-law Elizabeth to the dump to gather firewood, she asked them also to look around for wire which she could use to make a chicken pen.

"My brother and sister-in-law allowed me to tag along. While they were looking around, I exclaimed, 'See what I have found! A box of books!'

" 'Oh, Nellie, you bookworm!' Perfecto laughed. 'Those books are wet from the storm.'

" 'Here are some that look interesting,' I coaxed. 'I am going to take them home, especially this one. It says *La Santa Biblia*. It must be in Spanish.' "

As Nellie recounted to me the events of that happy day in her life, she said, "We did not know the meaning of the words *La Santa Biblia,* but the book held a fascination for us. Later we learned it was a Spanish Bible, but we could not read it, because we had been educated in English. However, my sister-in-law and my sister Dolores were able to read to us. Evening after evening they read from what we called 'the book that talks about Jesus.'

"We did not know it at the time, but we were being influenced by that Book to prepare to meet our Lord.

"In 1931 some Christian neighbors, Maude and Aaron Silva, came to our home and helped us study the Bible. What a beautiful revelation to learn that salvation is free; we had been redeemed by the blood of Jesus. As we read the Bible and studied together, and later attended evangelistic meetings, one by one the members of my family gave their hearts to the Saviour.

"The first of our family to be baptized were my sister Dolores and her husband Felix Chavez. Then Rosa and her husband Henry Riveras soon followed their example, as did my brother Perfecto and his wife, Elizabeth, and my sister Isabel and her husband, Alberto. Soon my sisters Juana Mazon and Eliza took their stand, but Anna Gallardo, my mother, did not become a baptized member until several years later.

"As the years passed, my sister Rosa and her husband Henry reared their children in the blessed hope; but with the lack of Christian schools, along with worldly influences, the children and grandchildren were drawn away from God. Rosa's son, Ray, although baptized at the age of thirteen, married a Catholic girl, and their children were sent to a parochial school, where they were confirmed as Catholics. My sister Rosa, however, never gave up praying for her children and grandchildren. And the loving Father heard and sent His Spirit to speak through the unfolding experiences of life. Her life greatly influenced Ray Junior. He realized she possessed a security and inner peace that he and his wife reverenced and longed to have for themselves. Consequently, he suggested to his wife, Candy, during a time of depression, that she study with the Seventh-day Adventists. 'They really teach the Bible,' he assured her.

"As a result Candy joined the church and began to pray for Ray.

"In 1974 Ray became an active member of the church, and for a number of years served as caretaker for the Seventh-day Adventist campground in Prescott."

"In the life of my grandmother and great-grandmother Gallardo," Ray observed, "everyone saw Christianity at work. It seemed every person they touched felt lifted to a higher level. Every member of the family respected them. Bad habits were literally left outside the door. There was no drinking or swearing in the house, and rarely did anyone even smoke while there. Truly the life of both my grandmother and greatgrandmother had a profound influence over our family."

One of the amazing parts of this story is the fact that Rosa's and Nellie's great-greatgrandmother, born about 1836, observed the Bible Sabbath in Old Mexico, not knowing of anyone else in the world who did.

An Exciting Discovery

Vicenta Ochoa-Roman could hardly wait to tell the news to her husband Marcelino, her brother Mario, and her two sisters, Geronima and Concha. "You can't imagine what I have discovered." Her face beamed with enthusiasm.

"What have you discovered?" they chorused.

"Well, I have been reading *La Santa Biblia*," she replied.

Her husband drew in a deep breath. "Don't you know that is forbidden? We have been told that we cannot understand it. Are you sure you are doing right?"

"Well, *La Biblia* is very interesting, and you will be surprised with what I am finding," Vicenta defended herself.

"What, for instance?" her brother asked.

"Well, would you believe it? There seems to be nothing about penance," she declared.

"No penance?" they asked in surprise. "How do you know?"

"That is precisely what I want to tell you and see what you folks think. Let me read something to you; it is in 1 John 1:7. 'The blood of Jesus Christ his Son cleanseth us from all sin.' And verse 9 says, 'If we confess our sins, he is faithful and just to forgive us our sins, and to cleanse us from all unrighteousness.' What does that mean to you?" Vicenta challenged them. "I did not say that; it is in God's Word."

Her reasoning sounded so logical that the young people began an intensive search and found more and more ideas that made them hunger for greater light. The more they read, the more truth they found.

Soon they lost their fear of reading the Bible. Next they ventured into a Pentecostal church. On the way home the young people felt very enthusiastic—that is, all of them except Vicenta.

"The people were so friendly. I would like to return," Geronima remarked.

"Vicenta," Mario turned to his sister, "why were you turning the pages of the Bible during the sermon? Why didn't you listen to what the preacher was saying?"

"I was listening, probably better than you were," Vicenta defended herself. "He talked about an eternally burning hell where the wicked have been since the first sinners who died. Did you notice that? Tormented souls crying for 5000 years already and going on into eternity!"

"To be honest with you," Mario replied, "I didn't notice."

"Well, when we reach home I want to read something to you that I found just last week. I thought I had marked it in my Bible, and that is what I was looking for during the sermon," Vicenta told them.

After dinner the four young people gathererd to hear what Vicenta wanted to tell them. "The verse I found was in Ecclesiastes 9:5. Why don't you read it from your new Bible, Mario."

"For the living know that they shall die: but the dead know—" Mario read and then paused.

81

"Finish," Vicenta urged.

"Know not any thing!" Mario finished with an exclamation in his voice, then repeated, "know not *any thing*."

"Don't you remember that last week, as we were reading the Gospel of John, when we came to the story of Mary, Martha, and Lazarus, Jesus said Lazarus was asleep, when he was dead?" Geronima reminded them.

"Something has just occurred to me," Marcelino spoke cautiously, as though hoping for their approval. "If the dead are already in heaven or in hell, why should there be a resurrection?"

"You're right," they all agreed.

"Well, we will have to look for another church. We haven't found the right one yet," Mario declared.

By Tuesday evening Vicenta had made another revolutionary discovery, which she shared with the other members of the family. "Yesterday morning I started to read the Ten Commandments. They're found in Exodus 20. And it says the seventh day is the Sabbath. Ever since that time I have tried and tried to find where the day was changed to Sunday."

"What day?" Concha asked.

"The Sabbath day! Look at the calendar and you will see that *Sabado* is the seventh day, so it must be God's rest day, and 'in it thou shalt not do any work,' the Bible says. I fear we are not keeping the right day, and I am certain we do not keep Sunday the way the Sabbath was supposed to be observed. We wash, go to the store, hoe in the garden.

"Vicenta, don't tell us any more," Mario interrupted. "This is too radical a change in thinking. I can't stand any more today," Mario objected.

Vicenta kept her thoughts to herself and prayed

much during the following days as she went about her work. Then one evening Mario came home out of breath. "Vicenta," he gasped, "I have found a man who keeps the Bible Sabbath. He attends what is called the Seventh Day Church of God. Let's talk with him."

Vicenta, Marcelino, Mario, and Geronima then ventured to church with their newfound friend. How thrilled they were for a time; but as they studied at home together they began to find more light that opened the love of God to them in a new and deeper way. Their search to find a church that taught the whole Bible continued.

After much more searching, the young people exclaimed one memorable day, "Now we have found what we have been looking for—a church which teaches no penance; we have been redeemed by the blood of Jesus, who through the Holy Spirit makes it possible for us to live the life of an overcomer. There is no purgatory or an eternally burning hell. We have learned of the Bible Sabbath, and as though that were not enough, we now know the prophecies about the soon coming of Jesus, who will take us where all our hearts' desires will be realized! How blest we are!"

On a happy Sabbath day in 1918 Vicente, Marcelino, Mario, and Geronima were baptized and became members of the Seventh-day Adventist church in San Antonio, Texas.

In 1925 the family moved to Phoenix and found the Montezuma Avenue church family ready to welcome them. The other three family members who joined the church with Vicenta have gone to rest, but she still waits for Jesus to come. Vicenta still attends services, and through sickness and health, vicissitudes and blessings, she kept active until age took its toll.

A Dream Is Born

Adiel Sanchez spoke earnestly to his guest, Elder Ernest Bond, who was visiting the little company of believers in the settlement of Sanchez. "Since we learned the wonderful news of our redemption by the blood of Jesus and of His soon coming, I have a great burden to share this message with my Spanish-speaking people.

"As you know," Adiel continued, "Augustine, our oldest son, is working in Nogales and plans to dedicate himself to the ministry. But the boy needs more education. I also have more children I desire to give to the Lord for the spread of the gospel. What can be done to prepare them for this great work? I am deeply burdened.

"Here in Sanchez the school board consists of two of my brothers and me. Because of this, we have been able to hire Adventist teachers for the little school; but beyond the eighth grade there is no provision for Christian education."

Elder Bond spoke up. "This burden of the education of the Spanish-speaking young people has rested not only upon the hearts of you parents, but also the Arizona Conference and the General Conference. It has been suggested that we might be able to educate young people from other Spanish-speaking countries also, and then send them back as workers for God. The idea has been well received, and plans are under way. However, with the total membership of the Arizona Conference scarcely reaching the one-thousand mark, this is a tremendous undertaking. It will require a great step forward in faith. Six acres have been purchased for a school, and we plan to present the importance of this project to our people at the time of the annual camp meeting."

Lawrence Stump, one of the young people who attended that camp meeting, in recounting the experience, stated, "A blackboard divided into squares representing the amount of money needed to get the school started was placed up front. We remained there until all the squares had been filled by gifts or pledges before the meeting was dismissed."

As a result of the vision of the workers and church members, plans were laid to start a Spanish training school in Phoenix. Consequently, with little funds but great faith, the Spanish-American Training School was founded in the fall of 1920, with Henry Brown as principal.

While classrooms and dormitories were under construction, the students and many of the faculty lived in tents. Elder A. R. Sandborn, conference president; A. N. Allen, a long-time worker among Spanish-speaking people; Elder R. L. Benton, pastor of the Phoenix Central Church; and Elder Ernest Bond, then secretary of the Spanish work in the Southwest, took the lead in the development of this project.

In addition to the six acres originally purchased on what is now North Fourteenth Street, south of McDowell Road, several other tracts of land on or near McDowell Road were leased so that the school could operate a dairy and have land for gardens.

Lawrence Stump, who had been canvassing in the Douglas and Tombstone area since graduation from Southwestern Junior College, now Southwestern Union College, Keene, Texas, received a letter from Elder Sandborn asking him to fill the position of dean of men at the new school.

Lawrence attended the first faculty meeting, where plans for the school year were laid and teachers assigned their respective duties. To his amazement he found that besides being dean of men, he would teach several classes, be in charge of the operation of the school farm, the cafeteria, and store, as well as supervise the maintenance of the grounds.

"How can you do all that?" his wife, Irene, asked when he told her about his schedule.

"I don't know, Dear. But you should see the load some of the others are carrying," Lawrence defended the rest of the faculty. "Provisions must be made for the students to earn part or all of their expenses. The girls are to be taken daily to homes in the community to work for their board and room. Somebody has to go out and solicit jobs, provide transportation, and supervise their work. Mrs. Frances Nordberg is looking after the girls. I wouldn't want her job.

"Classes begin at eight in the morning, so the school bus is to go out and gather the girls from the various homes at seven o'clock and have them at the school in time for classes, which will be dismissed again at noon so the girls can be returned to their various places of employment."

"What about the boys?" Irene asked.

"The ones I can't use on the farm, the dairy, the store, the cafeteria, and grounds maintenance will work at mechanics or help construct the new dormi-

tories. Oh yes, and there will be a school laundry,"
Lawrence continued.

"Are you in charge of that too?" his wife asked.

"No! I'm glad for that. They're hoping to find one of
the more mature students to take charge of that."

The harmonious integration of young people from
various parts of the world, many of them already with
set habit patterns in life, proved to be a gigantic task.
To teach them good study habits, social graces in a co-
educational atmosphere, the importance of presenting
themselves on time for classes and work assignments,
in addition to keeping before them the true goals of life,
at times overwhelmed the young faculty.

Glimpses of School Life

The study-work program at the school was occasionally interrupted by a day's outing on the riverbank. One time on the way back from one of the picnics, Augustine Sanchez's car ran out of gas, miles from a service station. "What shall we do?" they wailed. "The others have already gone ahead! Suppose we have to sit here all night while someone walks to town."

"And I hear they have javelinas out here!" One of the more fearful girls shuddered as she spoke.

"Augustine," one of the boys suggested, "there is a can of kerosene in the back of your car. Why don't you try putting it in the gas tank? Let's see how far it takes us." With much giggling and many misgivings the experiment was tried and proved to be a satisfactory way to get home. Fifty years later those who rode with Augustine that certain day still recounted the experience with zest.

Ildefonso Flores, although small of stature, rose to his full height as he stood in the doorway of the school laundry and voiced his objections to the assignment given him. "Do a woman's work! I earned a scholarship. Why should I scrub collars on a washboard? Why should I carry out the wash water by the bucketfuls?"

Agner Ann Romero, in charge of the school laundry,

feared for a moment that she was in for a battle royal, but after a few words with Ildefonso she was delightfully surprised to find that in spite of his sputterings, he carried on his assigned duties with a smile. This attitude carried him through many perplexities in his future life when he went as a Bible worker to New Mexico, Mexicali, Guadalajara, and Nogales. Returning to Arizona, he joined the corps of workers at Tempe Clinic-Hospital, where he remained for nine years before going to Paradise Valley Adventist Hospital in California.

Emma, age twenty-five, presented herself to Principal John D. Livingston for enrollment in the training school.

"How much education do you have?" Elder Livingston asked.

"I have never been to school," she replied.

"Can you read?" Elder Livingston asked.

"My mother died when I was thirteen, leaving me with my stepfather," she began, not answering his direct question.

"Where were you living at the time?" Elder Livingston asked in order to understand more fully the girl's background.

"In Coahuila, Mexico." Then she continued, "One day I decided to make some doll clothes, so I began hunting through a box of scraps of material. Hidden underneath all the pieces of cloth, I felt a heavy package. When I took off the wrappings, I found my mother's Bible.

"Just at the moment I had made the discovery, a colporteur walked into our home and stood looking over my shoulder. When he saw my great delight at finding the Bible he asked, 'Can you read?'

" 'Yes,' I assured him. 'That is the only legacy my dear mother left me. While she was sick, I sat by her bedside and she taught me to read.

"As soon as I had found the Bible, I had no more interest in doll clothes. The colporteur gave me a book entitled *Cristo Nuestro Salvador* [Christ Our Saviour]. I began reading Matthew, and read through the New Testament and the book that had been given me. By that time I had found the Sabbath. It was such a joy and comfort.

"In 1916 I was baptized in Torreon, Coahuila, by Elder G. W. Caviness, and now I have come to attend school." Elder Livingston allowed Emma to enroll and remain there for four years while she worked in people's homes and attended school. In telling us her story, Emma said, "One day Elders Bray and Fernandez urged me to go to care for the Regalado children, whose mother had died very suddenly. They really made a trap for me." She laughed as she spoke. "They insisted that if I did not care for those children they might be killed or lost eternally. There were five of them, ranging in ages from six months to eleven years. The baby, Sarah, clung to me like I was her mother. You see, I married Mr. Regalado."

The majority of the young men who attended school had their eyes focused on service in the spread of the gospel. They naturally looked for wives who would be compatible with the type of work they had chosen. Apparently there were instances when even the teachers cooperated in making wise choices or giving advice, because we learn that one day Elder Henry Brown suggested to Carlos Ayala that Agner Ann Romero would make a good wife. Carlos replied, "Oh, no. She has already refused me. She is in love with a cousin."

When the cousin came to the school, he gave a talk against religion. In fact, he was practically an atheist. This settled the question in Agner Ann's mind. But in the meantime, Carlos had begun to give his attentions to Carolina Salazar, so Augustine Sanchez started cultivating the friendship of Agner Ann. The two young men were so mixed up in their love affairs that people for a time did not know which girl was being courted by whom.

Happy memories also centered about the Sabbath. In the afternoons when the students and teachers went out to give Bible studies in the homes, precious experiences resulted. To their everlasting joy they saw the results of their work in baptisms of precious souls.

Under the principalship of A. N. Allan, the student body reached 125 during the 1923-24 term. It was composed of young people from many different places—Arizona, New Mexico, Texas, and Old Mexico.

Among the students sponsored by the Mexican Union Mission were Columba Zarate-Ortiz and Andrea Plata-Chavez, who had canvassed and ingathered for missions all over the republic. In appreciation for the faithful work the girls had done, the Mexican Union obtained passports and assisted them in getting started in school. Andrea and her husband, Cayetano Chavez, later returned to Mexico as missionaries.

J. A. Salazar, who came to the school from the South Texas Conference, gave forty-two years of service to the cause of God—thirty-one in Mexico and eleven in the United States.

The first young man to be ordained to the gospel ministry from among the students was Augustine Sanchez, from whose family have come numerous workers.

Brother Christian Shultz, a little-known German colporteur who traveled from pueblo to pueblo in Mexico, sold a *Señales de los Tiempos* (Signs of the Times) to Francisco Zepeda, a carpenter, in Pachuca, Hidalgo, Mexico.

Francisco began to study with his wife, Marciana. Then he shared the newly discovered truth about the Sabbath with his friend Antonio Sausa. Antonio promptly went to his sister, Mrs. Andres Perez, a devout Catholic. He appealed to her that she owed it to her children to study the Word of God for herself. She soon became convinced of the Sabbath also, as did her husband, who later spent twenty-eight years as a colporteur.

Mr. and Mrs. Andres Perez had four children. Enriqueta, the older daughter, attended the Spanish—American Training School and married Adiel Sanchez, Jr., whom she met at the school. Adiel Junior and Enriqueta spent some time in Chihuahua, Mexico, as missionaries, working with Elder Ernest Pohle. Their son, Albert, is a graduate of the School of Health at Loma Linda, California. He has taught six years in Montemorelos University in Mexico and now is with the School of Health again.

I Am a Preacher

Little did *Tio* (Uncle) Ricardo, the mail carrier for Sanchez, Arizona, imagine he was playing a part in pioneering the work of the Seventh-day Adventist Church in the twin cities of Nogales, Arizona, and Nogales, Sonora, the day he called at the Sanchez ranch, "Adiel, where are you?"

Tio Ricardo's voice echoed through the ranch house as he stepped inside, mail bag over his shoulder. "You had better open this important-looking letter addressed to Augustine."

Americans were troubled that summer of 1916 about the ominous news from the war in Europe, now known as World War I. "Is it from the draft board?" Adiel asked, as he reached for the letter.

"No. It says on the envelope Arizona Conference of Seventh-day Adventists, " the mail carrier replied.

Hurriedly the letter was opened. Various members of the family had gathered around to hear the news. It spread rapidly through the little settlement after the message had been read and reread and thoroughly discussed by the family—brothers, sisters, aunts and uncles, as well as the fond parents. Augustine was being asked by Elder Ernest Bond, conference president, to go to Nogales. There he would work with Fred Owens, assisting Elder Philip Knox in conducting an evangelistic effort.

In this close-knit family, Augustine's appointment was a momentous event. He was to be their first gift to the work of the Lord. The family members rejoiced at this.

The day before his twentieth birthday, August 17, 1916, the entire family, including all the relatives living nearby, assembled early. Each member determined to give Augustine a wonderful farewell. After waving and shedding a few tears of joy, accompanied by best wishes and many words of counsel from the family, Augustine left in a wagon for Solomonville, where he caught the train to Bowie. From Bowie to Tucson he traveled and then transferred to the Southern Pacific train which took him to Nogales, Arizona.

At the border, Augustine followed the crowds crossing the line over into Mexico, intending to find hotel accommodations on the Mexican side of Nogales. Striding along with two heavy suitcases, one in either hand, he came face-to-face with a guard who looked up at him and commanded, "Halt!"

Although Augustine spoke fairly good English, *Halt* was a new word to his vocabulary, so he proceeded forward, ignoring the order.

"Halt!" the guard shouted with a little more emphasis, but Augustine strode on.

"Halt!" The now-excited guard yelled the command, leaping in front of Augustine and shaking a huge rifle in his face.

Augustine dropped his bags, grabbed the rifle, and brushed the little guard aside.

Instantaneous pandemonium followed, with Augustine the center of the excitement. Border patrol and immigration officials descended upon him, seizing the rifle and returning it to the guard. Then they rushed the stranger and his bags into an inner office. Each official apparently drew his own conclusions about this young man, and each became a self-appointed inquisitor.

"Who are you? Where did you come from? Where are you going?" A volley of questions was thrown at him. And before Augustine could reply, another shouted, "Oh, we know who you are. You are a draft dodger!"

"I am a preacher; I am not a slacker," Augustine protested.

In the meantime the man in uniform who had first grabbed him opened his luggage and thoroughly ransacked it. In the process, he found Augustine's well-used Bible and the letter from the Arizona Conference, signed by Elder Ernest Bond, directing him to go to Nogales.

After the very frightened young man had satisfied the immigration authorities that he was a reliable citizen, they allowed him to proceed. Two days later, Fred Owens arrived with some of the equipment for conducting the evangelistic tent meetings, and together the two men began to lay groundwork for the arrival of Elder Knox and the meetings.

"We must find the best possible location on the American side, one that Elder Knox will approve," Fred Owens remarked.

They found what they thought to be an ideal spot on which to pitch the tent, just north of the Santa Cruz County courthouse, which overlooks the city of Nogales on the American side. "The tent is on the level of the city, so people won't have to climb the hill where the city hall is located, but every time people look toward the courthouse, they will see the *carpa* [tent]." Elder Knox arrived, and the meetings progressed. The people who came learned much of the glad news of the gospel. Then Halloween arrived, and the devil decided to take a hand in the whole affair. About a hundred mischief-makers surrounded the tent shouting, "Let's tear this thing down!" Some of the ringleaders grabbed the guy ropes preparatory to cutting them. In a mixture of Spanish and English, Augustine pleaded with them not to carry out their plans. While he was talking to the mob, the police arrived and carried the rabble-rousers away in paddy wagons. The meetings continued successfully. At the close of the meetings sixteen persons were baptized.

Augustine Sanchez and Fred Owens decided to move the tent to the Mexican side and hold another series on their own. The young men found a vacant lot near the Catholic church and set up their equipment. Soon they noticed light bulbs were missing from the tent, and hymnals and equipment disappeared. Fred and Augustine talked the matter over and decided that they should take turns sleeping on guard. However, Augustine suggested that since he was single, he would sleep in the tent.

The idea proved beneficial to their work, because since he remained at the tent after the services, it gave Augustine the opportunity to build friendships with those who cared to remain for a while to ask questions and discuss more fully the topics that had been presented. However, sometimes it would be eleven o'clock before the interested ones went home and Augustine could put down his bedroll on the platform, hang his clothes on a chair, and drop off to sleep.

On one occasion, in the wee hours of darkness, Augustine heard the tent flaps being moved, but due to his great weariness, he aroused only enough to pull the blanket over his head and glide back into unbroken slumber. However, a great shock awaited him in the morning. His suit, shirt, shoes, watch, and even his Bible were gone! What could he do? His room was on the American side of the border, three miles away. How he wished Fred Owens would come to his rescue with some clothes. All day Augustine endured hunger pangs, which finally drove him to scrounge through things that had been pushed under the platform. An old, abandoned pair of trousers never looked more beautiful. They had belonged to his co-worker, who was considerably shorter than he. Barefooted and shirtless, with pants far too short, Augustine waited until after dark before he stole across the border to his room.

The little flock in Nogales dwindled after the young men were sent elsewhere, and there was no regular pastor to care for them.

In 1927 Elder Clarence E. Moon organized a church in Nogales, on the American side. The group met in the United Fellowship Hall, a two-story, triangle-shaped building on Grant Street. There were still a few faithful Sabbath keepers meeting for worship in the same building about two years later.

About 1940 Elder Francis Games held evangelistic meetings in Nogales, which gave new life to the little church. However, the greatest blessing came when the offices of the Mission del Pacifico were transferred from Hermosillo, Sonora, to Nogales, Sonora, in 1956. From that date forward the work of God has spread in almost incredible ways.

In 1979 Carmen and Luis Ibarra, with the assistance of others, began to work toward the development of a group of Spanish-speaking people on the American side of the border. It was a matter of stepping out in faith, as only eight persons joined the group at the beginning.

By March 14, 1981 two acres of land had been purchased for a future building site, and the church had fifty-four active members.

We touch history superficially with only the tips of our fingers. Angels have recorded every prayer, each sigh, each victory for Christ. Soon we shall learn from them and from firsthand stories told by the redeemed the accounts of their progress and final rescue from this world of tears and heartaches into the kingdom of eternal glory.

The Impossible!

Elmer McCormack, a landscape gardener in Tempe and a member of the Tempe Seventh-day Adventist Church, had a great desire to see some work done among the Spanish-speaking people who lived on the north side of the city.

Everyone seemed too busy. Finally Brother McCormack, in desperation, said, "If someone will lend me his Spanish Twentieth Century Bible tapes and the filmstrips that go with them, I will see what I can do myself."

Brother McCormack could not speak Spanish, but he was dedicated and had a great desire to see that the Spanish-speaking people heard the message he loved so dearly.

And he succeeded.

Shortly after beginning the studies he had a group of people ready to attend church services. Some of the English-speaking members from the Tempe church decided to help Brother McCormack. They started a branch Sabbath School, which they held in a Baptist church in Scottsdale.

Daniel Parra, maintenance man at Thunderbird Academy, became very interested in this new work started by Brother McCormack. With Dan's leadership ability, together with his wife Carmen's help, the work has grown to a well-regulated church organization with sixty-three members, who now have an increasing savings account toward a church building of their own.

A very touching part of the Sabbath morning service, the day the author visited the Tempe Spanish church, was just before the close of Sabbath School. One by one members came forward, presented a thank offering, and expressed their appreciation for some personal blessings. Among the gifts presented there was not a coin—all paper money.

I thought to myself, "I might have had part in getting this wonderful group started, but I was too busy!" Is there today something we should be doing in the work of spreading the gospel, but find ourselves too busy? What sad words, "It might have been!"

This happy and enthusiastic company of Spanish-speaking Sabbath keepers was organized into a church August 16, 1975.

A Soldier for Christ

Daniel Parra, greatgrandson of a French soldier of fortune in the army of occupation under Maximilian in Mexico, and grandson of a Yaqui Indian girl, and now a member of the Tempe Church, told us this story.

"During the time I was in Nogales, Sonora, in 1948, I purchased a book by Ellen G. White on health. With it came eighteen lessons, which I studied. The book and the lessons made a great impression upon my life and prepared me to accept more instruction regarding better living as God sent it. The facts I learned from that book were etched in my mind, and many questions I had were answered. I learned that God is interested in our physical well-being. Also I found that He is able to speak to us spiritually when we have clear minds and healthy bodies."

"Carmen," I asked Dan's wife, "what started you in search of Bible truth? Where did you first learn of the Sabbath and Jesus' soon coming?"

Carmen unfolded a real-life drama as thrilling as a mystery story. "My grandmother was a student nun and my grandfather a student priest. They fell in love, and so they left the convent and began studying the Bible. Naturally, their homelife was different because they did not depend upon what they were told, but upon what they found in the Holy Scriptures. That is the background into which my father was born—where the parents thought independently for themselves and read the Bible.

"In Nogales, Sonora, my father heard of people who studied and taught only the Bible, so he attended their meetings and found them to be Seventh-day Adventists. Soon my father pressured us children to attend the same meetings and to keep the Bible Sabbath.

"It was hard to break away from the customs of all our friends while living in a Catholic community. To add to my perplexities, I met Dan, who was Catholic. We were friends for about two years before he went to San Luis Obispo, California. I prayed a great deal about our future. Should I terminate the friendship with Dan and learn more about the things my father was trying to teach us, or marry Dan as a Catholic?

"Finally my love for Dan won out, and on December 21, 1954, against my father's wishes, Dan and I were married in the Catholic church in Nogales, Sonora. My parents did not even attend the wedding, they felt it so keenly. Later we were married by the civil authorities also, as is customary in Mexico. Then we went to live in San Luis Obispo, where we met a couple by the name of Jim and Ivy Baughman. They took a great interest in us and week after week took us to church, until we fully accepted the beautiful message of salvation.

"Since we have both become Seventh-day Adventists, the Lord has richly blessed us. We have five children, all serving the Lord and planning to fill their places in finishing the gospel so that very soon we can go home to be with Jesus."

At the time of the publishing of this book the Parras are working at Thunderbird Academy. Carmen is the school nurse and Dan is in charge of maintenance.

My Husband's Secret

Heidi Cruz smiled as she said, "Suppose you had been married to a Seventh-day Adventist for many years and didn't know it? That is what happened to me."

"First I should explain my own attitude toward religion. For thirty-nine years of my life I was completely dedicated to Catholicism. All our children were baptized in the church, we attended mass regularly, and when anyone who had anything to do with any other church came to our door, I did not even talk with them. But God has ways of reaching the heart.

"One Sunday morning I found a radio program entitled 'La Voz de la Esperanza' (The Voice of Prophecy), which I liked so well that as soon as mass was over each Sunday I hurried home quickly to turn on the radio. I listened to the messages and then ordered the free Bible correspondence course. When I received the last lesson, a colporteur came to our door.

"I did not even want to allow the colporteur to enter our home, because I was aware that he was a Protestant. So, like any good colporteur, he stood outside and talked until finally we invited him inside. After we had ordered the books he was selling, he asked us whether we were listening to 'La Voz de la Esperanza.' And I told him I listened every week after mass.

"As the colporteur called to make collections for the payments on the books, he offered to give us Bible studies. And that is how I had the first personal contact with the Seventh-day Adventist Church.

"I was surprised how much my husband knew about the Bible as we continued to take studies. Then he finally told me his secret. He had been baptized a Seventh-day Adventist when he was fourteen years of age. I don't know how he kept the secret from me for so long. He confessed to me that he had left the church when he went into the army. He had never mentioned it, except that when I began taking the Voice of Prophecy lessons, he told me, 'They teach the truth.'

"It is as I told you at the beginning—God has ways of reaching hearts, and He did so in such a tactful way that now we are united in our service to Him. It was not as in some sad cases where one pulls one way and the other another way.

"Brother Victor Cancel is the faithful colporteur who began giving us Bible studies. Week after week he came, sometimes very tired, but each Friday evening for about a year he was there. All this time my husband was working on the Sabbath. Occasionally the children and I would go to church. I prayed a great deal before making the change because I did not want to lead my family into error.

"In the fall of 1967 Eugenio, my husband, and I together made our decision to serve God and were baptized. Thanks to God, our children were all educated in church school. Three have married, all in the church. I have so much for which to thank God. It was difficult to change my way of life after so many years; but once an individual has found the joy and peace of heaven in following the Bible, there is nothing else to do but obey."

My Guardian Angel Awoke Me

"I heard my guardian angel call my name. That was what first turned me to the Lord," Art Lopez spoke with determination.

"A Seventh-day Adventist dairyman named Ezra Nash hired me, and as we worked he always talked about the Lord. I paid very little attention until one day I noticed that out in the world where I was living certain things started to happen to me, and this caused me to ask myself the reason.

"The first thing to shake me up was that I began falling asleep during the twenty-mile drive home from work, and each time I would be about ready to drive off a bridge or get into some other dangerous situation, a voice would call, 'Arturo, wake up!' I believe that was my guardian angel. After this happened every night for two weeks, I said 'Lord, if You care that much for me, I will listen.'

"Then I began to take Bible studies from Ezra Nash. After almost a year I was prepared for baptism by Elder Lyndon DeWitt. I thought Elder DeWitt was very thorough, but he wanted to be certain I knew the importance of remaining true to God. As a matter of fact, I thought he was too strict and left the classes twice, but then I prayed about it and realized he was right.

The third time I came back and stayed.

"Ezra kept telling me, 'Art, since you started studying, my family and the whole church in Chandler have been praying for you every day.'

"While hauling hay to Tucson, it was the custom of truckers to stop at Picacho, drink coffee, and check our loads to be sure they were not loose. On one particular day I decided not to stop. About five miles east of Picacho I fell asleep. I had a forty-foot trailer loaded with baled hay. The great danger in falling asleep is that those huge rigs jackknife and turn over, and the driver is killed. I was headed off the highway when I fell asleep. In that instant a voice said, 'Art, wake up!' When I realized the situation, my first instinct was to turn quickly back toward the highway; but the voice spoke, 'Don't do it! Step on the gas and keep going straight.' So I did.

"The whole truck flew off the freeway and plowed into the sandy shoulder. Swift as an arrow that truck righted itself mysteriously, and I was able to guide it back onto the freeway. I did not even lose a bale of hay. As I continued traveling toward Tucson, I realized I was alive by a real miracle and that there was something the Lord wanted me to do. It must have been the prayers of the church members that had again saved my life.

"The next hurdle I had to cross was giving up cigarettes. I had smoked three packs a day for seventeen years. One morning I bought two packs, took one with me to work and left one on the table at home. I told Ezra, 'When I smoke these two packs, then I am not going to smoke anymore.'

" 'There is no compromise with the Lord for doing things that way,' he told me. So I never smoked another cigarette. Now when I listen to people telling of their struggles, and even of going through the Five-Day Plan, I thank God that He took the desire from me in one day. God did the same for me with liquor. I used the beer on hand to mix with poison for the flies at the dairy.

"My wife is also a faithful Seventh-day Adventist and so are her sisters and my daughters. We are looking forward to a big family reunion in heaven."

A Friend Invited Me

"How did I find the Lord?" Maria Gutierrez replied to my inquiry by repeating the question and then followed with the answer. "Nobody talked to me about my personal salvation, except the Holy Spirit put a great longing in my heart to grow closer to God. I thought I was searching for Him, but I later learned that He had been calling me by working out circumstances to help me recognize His guiding hand.

"After my marriage I began to read the Bible and attend the Catholic Church regularly. Still my heart felt starved for something I could not find.

"A short time later I met a Baptist friend who talked to me about the Bible in a way I had never heared before. She too had been a very devout Catholic, but when she began to read for herself she felt the Lord guided her as she asked for understanding. Her experience really interested me, because I had not heard anyone talk so beautifully nor had I met anyone who felt so much as I did. Then she said to me, 'There is going to be a conference tonight. It is not of my religion, but they speak of very beautiful themes, and it is in Spanish.'

" 'That is just what I need!' I exclaimed. 'Are you going?'

" 'No,' she replied, 'because my children are too small. However, I have a friend who is going. She can pick you up.'

"I am glad I agreed to go, although I did not know this lady, Hermalinda Lopez, was an Adventist. What I heard that night thrilled me. Afterward I told my husband about it and assured him I had heard things more beautiful than I had ever heard before. He was alarmed when I told him Pastor Ramon Espinoza's sermon was on the mark of the beast. My husband said the Protestants were putting ideas in my head. I assured him they were only reading what is in the Bible, and from what I had heard the night before, we need to understand what is about to happen in the world, or we will be surprised when the prophecies begin to be fulfilled.

"My husband was not very well pleased when I arranged to take Bible studies from Pastor Vasquez, but he did not oppose me very much. Guess what he did! He stayed in another room. But after about three Bible lessons, he began to sit with us, as did some of our neighbors.

"It was a real joy to us when Sister Hermalinda told us that there is a church where they speak Spanish and where they teach the same beautiful things from the Bible we had been hearing.

"Of course I shared the wonderful message with my two sisters Alicia Rubalcaba and Guadalupe Trombley, who now also rejoice in the same blessed hope of seeing Jesus soon."

Worth Everything

A member of the Tempe church suggested that I talk with Alicia Rubalcaba. "Alicia," the member said, "has an interesting story to tell of how she found the Lord."

This is the story Alicia told: "During the time I was becoming acquainted with my Lord and learning to do His will, I not only felt the heartbreak of my husband's disapproval and rejection, but also the trap my friend set for me which made me feel like a condemned martyr."

"A trap! How did that happen?" I exclaimed.

"That's a long story," she replied. "First I probably should explain that for some time I had felt a great spiritual hunger. I went through the exterior motions of being a good Catholic but began to read the Bible. Of course, I asked questions, but received no satisfactory answeres that harmonized with the teachings of the Holy Scriptures.

"One day my sister asked me to go to a meeting to be held in her home. I said No. But she insisted this was a very different meeting. Of course, I did not tell my husband, because I knew it would be like having a bomb explode. However, I went and took two others with me.

"I will never forget the beautiful lesson about repentance given by Pastor Manuel Vasquez. When he had finished, we begged him for more. He said he had an appointment which followed immediately, but if we wanted to hear more we should come back the next week. Of course we all wanted more, as I said, so we attended other classes and then evangelistic meetings in the church. After each meeting my heart was filled with a heavenly joy. I felt my soul had been fed, after being hungry for so long.

"The more I learned, the more I wanted to know and the more I wanted to share the marvelous news with my dear husband.

"When the day finally came that I had the courage to tell him I was going to follow the beautiful message I had heard, the poor fellow was so shocked that he wept for three days and nights and did not eat or sleep. He would come home from work and we would begin to talk and discuss my intentions. On and on we would talk until it was time for him to go to work again. We even talked of divorce. He threatened that if any of the pastors from the church came to our house he would throw them out. He, as well as I, really suffered a great deal because we really love each other.

"When Pastor Ramon Espinoza began to hold meetings, I coaxed my husband to attend. How thrilled I was to sit beside him and listen to the beautiful lesson presented that first night. The next day, who should come to our door but Pastor Espinoza. I invited him in, trembling and wondering what would happen. But he and my husband had a very nice conversation. After that each Sabbath morning I would slip out of the house to attend church so as not to disturb my husband's rest, because he worked nights.

"I felt everything in our home was going much better

than I had even dared to hope. Then one terrible day a former friend came to visit, and that is when the trap was set for me. She refused to go to church on Sabbath morning, but remained at home.

"When I came in from church, it was as though my world had completely changed. The home atmosphere was charged with hostility. What had my friend done to me? I was soon to learn the trap she had set.

"As I started to change my clothes before warming and serving the food which I had prepared on Friday, my husband said, 'Don't change your clothes. We have an appointment.' I asked him what the appointment was. He replied, 'With the priest.' The bitterness in his voice made me catch my breath. Then it dawned upon me what they were planning—he and my friend. I must confess that all the peace and joy I had felt instantly fled. How could I survive this experience alone? In a frenzy I called my sisters. 'Pray! Please pray! I am in deep trouble!' was all I could say.

"I had always held such reverence and respect for the priesthood. How could I face an encounter with the man I had called father and to whom I had confessed the secrets of my heart? How could I tell him I had found something so much more satisfying? I shook like a leaf all the way there.

"Then something wonderful happened. I experienced the power of God in greater measure than I had ever known before. In the first place, this so-called friend spoke to the priest in English, and wonder of wonders I could understand. She told him that I was joining the Adventist Church because we have three retarded children and I wanted them healed. For that reason, she said, the Adventists had ensnared me because they pretend to heal people. I was able to reply to her accusations, and God gave me such composure that I was able also to explain to the priest that I had learned more from the Word of God during the past weeks than I had since my childhood. In addition to this, I told him that his church teaches us to adore a man here on earth in place of God, our heavenly Father. This I could no longer do.

"The priest did not pray with me; he did not read the Bible. He only accused me of leaving for personal benefit.

"I felt keenly hurt to think that someone I thought was my friend would influence my husband in such a manner that I would be treated as though I were a criminal.

"Fortunately the friend left, but those were very perplexing days in our lives and in our home. One day my husband went outside and wept like a child, and I went out and wept with him, because I love him very much. Finally, I told him it would be better for us to separate than live quarreling over religion. I agreed to take the three retarded children and to give him the youngest boy as my gift of love. All my poor husband could say was, 'Why did this happen to us?'

"As a final hope in trying to save our home, I suggested to my husband that we read the Bible together, just the two of us," Alicia continued. "However, it did not benefit us as much as we had expected because we did not know how to study it. Then some ladies came, and it was so refreshing to listen to them find messages of hope all through the Bible. My heart went out to Jesus, and I asked for baptism.

"You ask whether it was worth the struggle we passed through," Alicia concluded. "Let me assure you it truly was, a thousand times and more, even in this present life, because now our home, thanks to our heavenly Father, is happy again. My husband attends

113

church and reads the Bible. We are looking forward to spending eternity with our four children, all well and happy. I am certain that then we will feel the price was small and will thank Him throughout eternity that He loved us and redeemed us by His precious blood.

Section Seven
Camp-Meeting Tales

Angelita Urbalejo's Story

"If you want to hear about how the work is growing and how it first began in the old Southwest, you must attend the camp meeting for Spanish-speaking people held at Prescott," I was told.

I went, armed with writing tablets, pencils, pens, and a tape recorder. What stories I heard! Stories of the old Southwest! Stories of cattle ranching, sheepherding, Indian raids, floods, posses—they are nothing compared to the stories of the triumph of truth and its growth. The roots of Adventism go deep, and because of the depth of the root system, the growth to-day flourishes. "Like a tree," the psalmist says, "planted by the rivers of water." This is the story of that tree's root system started so many years ago, as told to me at camp meeting in Prescott, Arizona, in 1980—almost a hundred years after the first church was organized in Sanchez.

"Be sure you talk to Angelita Urbalejo," someone suggested. "She's ninety-six years old, the oldest member of the Tucson church."

I found her walking hurriedly across the camp-ground toward the main meeting place.

We found a bench to sit on while she told me high-lights of her eventful life which began in Riodosa,

Texas, August of the year 1885.

"My first husband, Emelecio Baldenegro, worked in the mines from 1917 to 1936. It was while he was working at Copper Hill near Globe that a friend of mine named Elena, said, 'Oh, you should hear the beautiful things a book salesman named Carlos Benitez is teaching.' We attended one of the Bible classes. We were so thrilled we never wanted to miss another. Our lives became completely changed.

"When we began to keep the Sabbath, we faced a great test of our faith in Jesus. The mining company refused to allow my husband to keep God's Sabbath. So we went to Phoenix and picked cotton for a while. Finally my husband found employment in a mine at what is now a ghost town in New Mexico.

"When we went to New Mexico we longed for friends who also kept the Sabbath. The Texico Conference finally sent Brother Wilson. Then later they sent Brother José Ortega, a colporteur, who spent three years selling books and preaching the gospel. That is how he found the Martinez family of Rancho Grande— the family written about in the book, *Three Angels Over Rancho Grande*."

During the time Brother Ortega remained, he won many souls to the Lord."

"My husband's lungs gradually filled with dust from the mines until he became so acutely ill that on May 22, 1936, we left everything—our home and furniture— and went to Tucson seeking medical care. We arrived there penniless. My husband died June 22, 1936.

"God has been so good to us. I have never suffered from hunger. We had thirteen children, but only three remain. I look forward to having my children with me in heaven."

Sister Urbalejo's son, Ed Baldenegro, standing

nearby, gave us a few very interesting touches to his mother's life. "After going through a full series of Bible lessons, my parents were baptized by the colporteur, Carlos Benitez, later by Elder Burt Bray in Tucson, because they learned that Brother Benitez was not an ordained minister.

"As a child I recall my mother's insistence that we children gather each night to study and pray. I thank the Lord for a mother who believed that Bible study is a must."

Sister Urbalejo has been doubly rewarded for her faithfulness in rearing her children. At the present time her son, Ed Baldenegro, who gave such a beautiful touch to his mother's story, is a real missionary. He and his wife drive many miles every week to assist in the operation of the little church at Oracle. During the past year he has been responsible for four souls being added to the church by baptism.

My Father's Prayers

David Ochon told me that he was born into a family of Seventh-day Adventists. "My parents," he said, "learned the message of salvation through some dear people in Empalme, Sonora, Mexico, who taught them to study the Bible.

"The amazing part is that when the people came to share the Bible with my father's mother and brothers, my father would go out the back door. Later, from curiosity he began to listen, without allowing anyone to know. His inquisitiveness finally led to a fascination for Bible study, which culminated in his baptism.

"My parents resolved to rear their family as Sabbath-keeping Christians. I am the eldest of ten children, all of whom were reared in the hope of a soon-coming Saviour. My ambition was to be a doctor, but due to problems which I encountered in school, I began to look to men instead of God, and thus was born a rebellious attitude in me.

"After leaving school, I tried to find work, but it proved to be very difficult. The harder it was to find work, the more bitter I grew. In the end I became a professional baseball player."

"After meeting the girl who later became my wife, I continued to travel with the baseball team. My father began at once to present Bible truths to the girl.

"At this time a miracle occurred in answer to my father's prayers. To me it was a tragedy. Our team was in practice for playing ball in Mexicali when suddenly the ball fell from my hand, and I was unable to raise my arm. The manager of the team ran to me, examined me, and sent me to a doctor. No one could find the cause of the problem. It cost me great anguish to give up my career.

"My sweetheart had the courage to go ahead and marry me in the face of all these problems. After we were married, I decided to come to the United States, because I have a brother and sister here, and I wanted to be near them. Since I was the only one of the ten children who was not serving God, it was good for me to be with them. I went alone, planning to have my wife come later. I had resolved to return to the ways of the Lord and keep the Bible Sabbath, but I did not tell anyone.

"After being in the United States for two weeks, my wife called me from Mexico to ask permission to be baptized. My reply was No. But I asked her to come to me immediately.

" 'What shall I do?' my wife asked my father.

"Reluctantly he replied, 'If David has said you may not, there is nothing we can do. You go to him and convince him to give himself to the Lord. Be brave, my daughter.'

"When she arrived in California, I told my wife the reason I had refused to allow her to be baptized—because I wanted to be baptized with her. Two weeks later we were baptized together.

"When we wrote home and sent pictures of our baptism, my father could not contain himself for joy."

Little did any of us realize this would be David's last camp meeting on this earth. Due to an accident, he was laid to rest soon after. What a thrill awaits us on the resurrection morning as we see David greeting his family!

119

Faulty Valves and a Dutiful Son

"Now tell me, how did you learn the message of salvation?" I asked a young man who joined a group with whom I was chatting.

"Through an automobile," Raul replied.

Everyone laughed and nodded their heads.

"Oh, this sounds interesting," I exclaimed. "Let's hear more."

Raul Maldonado began: "When I was about eighteen years of age, I was working on my car, and the valves needed to be ground. I didn't have a large income, so I wanted to save as much as possible. I told my mother that I needed someone to work on my car and wondered whether there was a member of the family who was a mechanic and had the necessary tools."

" 'Your uncle Tito is just the one you need,' she said. 'I haven't seen him in years.'

" 'I will call him immediately,' I replied.

" 'Oh, not today!' Mother cautioned. 'This is Tito's rest day. He goes to church on Saturdays.'

"I thought aloud, 'That seems very odd. He goes to church on Saturday? Everybody goes to church on Sunday, if they go at all.'

"The next day I called my uncle Tito Rivera. Of course, he knew me by name and told me to feel free to come anytime so we could discuss my problem.

"Well, I went to see Uncle Tito. As I walked toward his workshop I noticed he was working on a valve, but he also had a book at his side, which I knew must be the Bible. He would turn a page and read something and then work on the valve again. It impressed me, but as I paused to watch him, a great battle went on in my heart. Did I want my car to be repaired badly enough to allow him to push his religion down my throat? At least that is what I feared he would do.

"My need of help won that day. So I walked toward Uncle Tito and introduced myself. He had not seen me in years, but received me kindly. As our conversation progressed, I learned he was a Seventh-day Adventist.

"My curiosity was great, and I wanted to ask him many questions. I was so afraid he would try to press me into this religion, however, that I casually remarked that I had studied with the Jehovah's Witnesses and with some Baptists. Uncle Tito also remarked very casually, 'Would you like to talk about the Bible?'

" 'Well, possibly someday,' I agreed.

"Of course Uncle Tito helped me get my car into running order again. Weeks went by. My fears of his pushing me had subsided. Then one day Uncle Tito came to the house and began talking to Mom and Dad. Soon he had them involved in a conversation about the Word of God. As their interest and curiosity grew, he suggested that, since they had so many questions he could not answer, he would like to bring someone who could. The following week Uncle Tito brought Pastor Dupertuis, who gave Bible readings to my three sisters, my mother and my father. They exchanged ideas, reading everything from the Scriptures, and my family eagerly studied. I did not. I merely listened from a distance, because I did not want to be changed, as doubt-

121

less many of us feel when we are being introduced to something new.

"Eventually as the discussions became more interesting, I came closer to the dining table where everyone was gathered, and before I realized it, I was one of the group. I studied for about three or four months. Then we attended evangelistic meetings at the church. There I heard again everything I had learned in the Bible lessons at home. My sisters and my mother were baptized at the close of the meetings. But my father and I were not. Pastor Dupertuis did not pressure me; he would just say, 'When you are ready, Raul, let me know.'

"Faithfully I went to church every Sabbath, and finally the Holy Spirit worked on my heart, and I committed myself to Jesus and was baptized Christmas Day, 1965."

"Had you met your wife then?" I asked.

"No."

"You met her at church?"

"Yes," he replied with a smile.

"That was a a good place to meet," I added.

Lupe, Raul's wife, smiled her approval.

"That is Margarita Felix." Raul turned to a young woman who had slipped in during our conversation. "She attended our wedding in 1970. Margarita and her husband were Catholic and were rather opposed to any Protestant church. We visited in their home at various times and talked with them every possible opportunity. We also tried to be an example of what a Seventh-day Adventist Christian should be. Eventually we began to share the gospel with Margarita and Manuel, her husband, through Bible-related subjects as we went with them on outings. It took quite a time before they were fully persuaded that they wanted formal Bible studies.

And there is quite a story that goes with that.

"Are you related?" I wondered.

"Yes, she is my sister-in-law. She finally wanted me to give her Bible lessons, and since I did not feel capable, especially because we were family, I got Brother Baldenegro to give her the studies. Then Margarita was baptized."

Turning to Margarita, Raul asked a leading question to carry on the story. "Were you and Manuel baptized together?"

"No. He came later," she quietly observed. And she told of her searching for light and peace and of the great opposition from her husband.

"My husband and I fought a terrible battle—a battle over all the teachings and customs of our childhood," Margarita began. "We had been staunch Catholics, assured and positive it was the only way of life. However, I began to feel a longing for peace of soul, and the more I sought it, the higher wall of prejudice Manuel built around himself. So bitterly and blindly did he defend his former way of life that he hid the Bible from me in order to keep our home from breaking up.

"While Manuel was at work," Margarita continued, "I searched the house until I found the Bible. Then how I studied it! But of course, I hid it again before he came home. Daily I prayed for faith and for more light. Then I had a great desire to attend church with Raul and Lupe. So one Sabbath I went while Manuel was at work. When he found out, he threatened me, 'If you go to that church, you will go out one door of this house and I will go out another. There are plenty of other young women who go to mass, and I will find myself another wife among them.'

"It was necessary for Pastor Dupertuis to give me Bible studies secretly. In spite of his help, I still felt the need of greater assurance that the Bible that Lupe and Raul studied actually contained the gospel. So I went to the Catholic church and bought a Bible from the priest. As I compared the two Bibles, it became very evident that they taught the same truth.

"One day," Margarita continued, "I telephoned the priest at the cathedral and asked him why the Ten Commandments in the Catholic Bible say to keep the Sabbath but we observe Sunday as the Sabbath. The priest replied that the Catholic Church has the right to change the Ten Commandments.

"That was a great revelation to me. I continued to pray for light and guidance. I did not want to make a mistake about something so important as our personal salvation. From time to time I would read a few verses from the Bible to my husband, after he learned I was still reading it. Then I asked Pastor Carlos Montaño to come to our home to talk with my husband. And do you know what my husband did? He hid!

"That same week I had a dream that assured me I should follow the light. Although I loved my husband very much, I reasoned that he did not have eternity to give me. It apparently meant sacrificing him or life with Jesus.

"Well, because I had the faith to follow my Saviour, He has now given me my husband in the church and the promise of eternal life for both of us."

"How did Uncle Tito get into this story?" I now asked.

Tito Rivera married the Landeros girl. After the marriage the girl's mother cried and cried, much to the dismay of her four sons.

"You would think Pauline was the only child she had," one son ruefully commented.

"Let's make a deal. We will take turns taking our

mother out every night," another son suggested.

"Where could we take her?"

"To visit relatives or to a theater. Just something to occupy her mind. If we don't she will soon die."

So it was agreed.

"I will take her tonight," Alvaro offered. "I saw some sort of religious lectures announced which deal with prophecies from the Bible. Then tomorrow night one of you can take her somewhere."

When Alvaro and his mother returned from that first meeting, her tears were dry. As they walked into the house, Mother Landeros hurried to the bookcase and began searching for something.

"What do you want, *Mamacita?*" Alvaro looked over her shoulder.

"My Catholic Bible. I want to see whether what we heard tonight was true," she replied.

"You won't know how to find it," Alvaro patiently reminded his mother.

"Well, will you take me back tomorrow night so I can find out?" she asked.

Alvaro hurried out of the room. He would have to clear that arrangement with his brothers, although it was exactly what he would like to do. He felt an urgency to learn more for himself.

The brothers laughed to themselves, thinking they had trapped Alvaro into doing their duty. But together Alvaro and Mother Landeros listened and learned about eternal life.

Soon Mrs. Landeros asked to be baptized and join the group of Sabbath keepers. It was natural that her first thought then should be Pauline and Tito, with whom she shared the good news—salvation a free gift, no penance, no purgatory, a soon-coming Saviour, and the blessed Sabbath.

The rest of the story we learned from Tito himself. "This story began a long time ago, because Pauline and I were married in 1934. God was patient and led us forward gently. It was not until 1963 that I finally took a firm stand to serve God and joined the church. That is why I was still studying at my work when Raul came to me to have his car worked on.

"You see, when Pauline wanted to share the gospel with me, I assured her I could not understand the Bible. I preferred to read other books that had no profit for me. Finally, Pauline suggested I begin with Matthew and read the New Testament. That is what I did. However, the subject that interested me more was why the Adventists keep Sabbath when the majority of other churches observe Sunday. So I concentrated on that point first. My interest grew as I began to find the Sabbath mentioned again and again in the New Testament. Then I went to the Old Testament. Of course I found the Sabbath from the very beginning in the Garden of Eden, all the way through the Bible to the last chapter of Revelation.

"Of course the next point in Christian growth would be to attend church, which I did, at first from curiosity. But I noticed immediately that when the pastors said anything, they used the Bible and read from it. They did not say, 'We think it is this way,' or 'Our church teaches it that way.' I learned the Bible gives the answers and that one text explains another. In other words, the Bible stands on its own feet. It does not need someone to tell us what it means. That opened up a new world of study to me. I learn more all the time and marvel at the beauty of the Scriptures. Truth is the unfolding of a perfect harmony from Genesis to Revelation."

Crying Over Answered Prayer!

Rosario Quiroz intrigued me with her story. "That poor colporteur! He will always be an unsung hero in my life, until I can meet him in heaven and thank him for what he did," she said, shaking her head.

"Why? What did he do?" I asked, anxious to learn.

"First, I guess you would say it was what he did not do." Rosario laughed. "He came to the Hacienda de los Cedros, Zacatecas, where we lived during the early 1950s. And that poor man tramped from house to house trying to sell Christian literature. Everyone's eyes were closed to anything that might come from the outside; they all thought they belonged to the only real church, and so did not want to hear anything else.

"I have often wondered whether the colporteur went hungry that day. If I could have known what joy he would give us and how his visit to the hacienda would entirely change my life, I would surely have insisted at least upon feeding him and speaking a few words of encouragement."

"What did the stranger do that changed your life, if no one bought anything and everybody sent him away without offering him even a tortilla?" By now I too was feeling sympathy for him.

"He left an enrollment card for free Bible correspon-

127

dence lessons from La Voz de la Esperanza [The Voice of Prophecy]. We filled out and mailed the card. I don't know why we did it, but when the lessons came, my brothers and sisters and I studied them.

"With inexpressible joy we learned that we could speak directly to the heavenly Father without having to go through priests, or even through the Virgin Mary. It seemed almost too good to be true. That was the most thrilling message I had ever heard, and in my heart was born a great desire to find the people who teach this wonderful truth. So the first prayer I ever spoke in my own words from my heart directly to the heart of God was, 'Help me to find the people of the Word.'

"My prayer seemed to me to be a hopeless request, because we were living among people whose worship was more pagan than Christian. There was absolutely no possible way for us to think of ever leaving the hacienda.

"How the miracle happened in 1955 I cannot explain, but very soon we moved to Saltillo in the state of Coahuila, where I continued to attend the Catholic church, always in search of something for which my soul hungered.

"One day as I was walking in a procession with a girl friend, in honor of a clay saint that was being transported from one place to another, I looked up and read 'Mission Adventista' on a little chapel. My heart almost stopped beating. Here was the fulfillment of my prayer, I was certain, so I dropped out of the marching group, hurried up to the little church, and rang the doorbell.

"The pastor and his wife lived in an apartment above the mission. She answered the door and invited me into their home. I cannot put into words the boundless joy that filled my heart. All my pent-up emotions suddenly burst into uncontrolled tears. I could not speak. Now I knew that when I prayed, God heard and answered. In a vague way I had felt that some day I would find this church, but now when my prayer was answered, I could only weep. The missionary's wife was very understanding and waited until I was able to talk. When I could control my tears, I explained why I had come.

"That day marked a new and wonderful way of life for me. The missionary's wife began teaching me first the beautiful story of salvation through the Word of God—that we are redeemed by the blood of Jesus and that we can open our hearts in prayer and God will hear and answer, just as though we were the only children He has on earth.

"As time went on, the missionary's wife taught my whole family lessons in health—exercise, good food, and happy thinking. Each new step made us feel closer to our Lord. It should have bound our family all closer together. But there were some who loved the ways of the world more than an eternity with Jesus. So even though we learned that this new way of life would add years to the average life, still some met the lessons taught by the missionary's wife with opposition. I went forward with many pressures and trials at the moment, but the years have proved that God's way is easiest and best, even in this life.

"Our lives changed completely. But a new problem arose—a problem over music. My two sisters and I had been singing popular music on the radio. Somehow the Holy Spirit impressed me that the type of music we sang was not pleasing to God, so I refused to sing anymore.

"After a time, my mother, one sister, and I were baptized. That was in 1957.

129

"The missionary's wife told us about the training school in Navajoa, Sonora. I became possessed of a new ambition—to attend an Adventist school. God opened the way for me to attend, and after two years, in 1959, I graduated. I returned to Saltillo to study nursing and midwifery at the university. After completing my course of study, I returned to Navajoa as dean of girls for two years. I did not dream where this would take me.

"One of the monitors who helped me and who loved me very much had an uncle whom she also loved deeply and called Papa. She decided to play cupid, and wrote to him about me. As a result he wrote, as she had suggested.

"The strange part—shall I call it a miracle?—is that I had had a dream while I was still working in Saltillo as a nurse. In this dream I saw my future husband from Montemorelos College. At the time of my dream, a doctor in Saltillo wanted to marry me, but since he was not a Christian, I prayed much about it. I felt assured that God had a person chosen for me and began to pray for him long before we met.

"Naturally, when I was introduced to Marcelino Quiroz, I felt the guiding hand of God. And when you hear the story of my husband's family, you will agree with me, I am certain."

It was natural to want to learn another thrilling chapter in the stories angels are keeping in the records of heaven. So I asked to talk with Marcelino too.

"My family is from the state of Oaxaca," Marcelino began, "from the little town of Chalcatongo of the Mixteca Alta. However, it was not there that the gospel light first reached us. My brother Pedro learned about the freedom of worshiping God without the images and saints while he was working in Cordoba, Veracruz.

"As soon as Pedro learned the good news, he returned home to bring it to us. My parents and brothers and I gladly accepted all he told us. First, he said, we should burn all our images. We were so excited by what Pedro told us that we wanted to learn more, so he sent for someone to come teach us.

"Brother Ladislao Arriaga came. But when word passed through the village that we had destroyed the images, the priest became very angry and stirred up a very bad persecution. They beat Brother Arriaga with sticks until they had almost killed him. They also planned to burn our house and all we had. My brother fled to Veracruz, but we remained in Chalcatongo. The only way we could survive was for my father to pretend not to be an Adventist.

"God did not forsake us. We prayed in secret. And now I am happy to tell you that there is a Seventh-day Adventist church of about eighty members in Chalcatongo, and my father is among them."

Marcelino is now a retired worker from the active gospel ministry. Retired? No! He and Rosario are helping to fill the present church building with happy souls who will drink daily from the wells of salvation, and someday gather around the throne of grace in the heavenly land.

The Proofs That Failed

Victor Cancel hated Seventh-day Adventists. "I cannot give you any reason for my feelings, except what I had heard others say. I was very active in the Presbyterian Church in Aguada, Puerto Rico. My mother was a spiritualist medium. When we were sick she had always sent us to the witch, or had the witch come to our house to make incantations.

"But in 1933 a woman and her daughter started a branch Sabbath School in their home not far from ours. With our home environment, it seemed strange that my father should attend these meetings, but he did and liked them. Then he invited me to go, but I told him, 'No thank you, I have my church.'

"Father challenged me, 'Why won't you go? Are you afraid?'

"Just to show my father that I was not a coward, I decided to go just once; but I was so prejudiced that I didn't like anything I heard.

"After the service was over, I walked along the beach and talked about the wonders of creation with the daughter of the lady who had conducted the meeting. Then I said, 'Well, I hear you Adventists say we Presbyterians have the mark of the beast. Is that right?'

"To my surprise, instead of looking angry, the girl smiled and replied, 'Well, Victor, that is a very good question.'

"We talked as we went back to her home. Then she began reading the Bible to me. I was very belligerent, but she so tactfully guided me in a presentation of the Sabbath right from the Scriptures that I was impressed.

"The very next Sunday at my church the minister sold me a catechism. With real enthusiasm I told myself, 'This is just what I need to fight the Adventists.'

"I went to my home and prepared to make my attack with a long list of texts to prove Sabbath was changed to Sunday. The more I studied, however, the more convinced I was that my idea was not biblical. I spent most of the night searching, and finally the next day in desperation I went to my minister for assistance. Of course, he had no answer from the Bible. He tried to make excuses. I could tell he was uneasy and resented my questioning him.

"What can one do if he is to be honest with himself and God? Against my will, I became a Seventh-day Adventist. I realized that in the judgment I would have to give account to God, not to my pastor.

"In August 1959 we moved to Tucson, Arizona, where I became a pastor-colporteur—part-time pastor and part-time colporteur selling Christian books. There were twenty-eight members in the church at the time we went there. By 1961 there were double that number."

After All Those Years

"Let me tell you about the conversion of my mother," Onesimo Gutierrez suggested. "Mother was born in Los Lentes, south of Albuquerque, New Mexico, in 1889. Her parents named her Susana. When she was of school age, she was sent to Albuquerque, where she lived in the dormitory of a government school. While there Mother found a Bible which she read diligently, and to her surprise found—all by herself—that the seventh day is the Sabbath.

"Mother's parents were very strict Catholics, so for many years, although she believed, she kept her discovery about the Sabbath hidden in her heart.

"After finishing school, Mother returned to Los Lentes and threw herself into the social life of the community. As with everything else she did in her life, she put all her heart into it. In fact, she loved to attend dances and engage in what she thought were good times to such an extent that she once declared, 'No one can take this way of life from me—only death.'

"In 1908, at the age of nineteen, Mother married my father, George Gutierrez, a colorful figure in the early life of the West. Men such as he are now found in books of history and adventure. In fact, we once saw our father depicted in a television drama of the Wild West.

"My daddy was *mayordomo* [manager] of a large hacienda, which covered the territory in New Mexico from the Rio Grande to the White Mountains in the northern part of the state. Part of Dad's work was chief of *caparrales* [superintendent of the herders] for sixteen camps, each camp with several thousand sheep. Cattlemen and sheep herders did not get on well, and sometimes there were bitter hostilities between them.

"My parents were both excellent marksmen. As an example of Mother's prowess, one day when my sister was ill, she expressed a desire for duck. Mother walked to the shore of the lake and with one shot beheaded a duck, which the dog retrieved.

"My father held the respect of the outlaws. One hair-raising encounter he had was on the day when the outlaws decided to hang Uncle Leopoldo. My cousin came running to our house shouting, 'They are going to kill my father!'

"Fortunately Dad's horse was already saddled. He had been shaving, and half of his face was still covered with lather. Away Dad galloped, lather and all. The outlaws had put the rope around Uncle Leopoldo's neck and were dragging him to be hanged, but just as they were jerking the rope that was around my uncle's neck, Dad cut the rope with a single shot. This terrified the outlaws, and they fled.

"My parents remained in Los Lentes until after the birth of their first two children, José and Gertrudes. Ten more children were born after they moved to Springerville in 1920, but only six lived to adulthood.

"About 1938 my mother had a very vivid dream in which she and my sister Flora, who had already died, were running from the devil. Tired and exhausted, they suddenly came to a dead end before a solid wall. In their desperation they stood wondering how they could get over before the devil could catch up with them. To their surprise they saw a Stranger standing beside them who asked, 'Why are you running?'

"As they gasped for breath Mother explained their plight.

" 'Don't worry,' the Stranger said, 'I am Michael the Archangel,'

"Mother quickly asked, 'How can we get over this high wall?'

" 'Don't worry,' the heavenly Being said again, and then added, 'I will make you small like ants. See that crack in the wall. Go through there, and on the other side you will see roads going to the right and to the left. Don't take them, but keep going straight ahead.'

"Was Michael telling them to leave everything of the world behind and to follow the straight and narrow way to heaven? That is apparently the way Mother understood it.

"Mother and Flora passed through to the other side of the wall. They looked around. It was a beautiful place. To their joy, Michael met them. As He looked upon them, He spoke in a voice filled with love, 'Sister, go and sin no more.' Then Mother awoke.

"The dream completely changed Mother's life. She apparently understood exactly what the heavenly Father was trying to tell her, for the very next morning she said to me, 'Son, today is the Sabbath of the Lord. We must keep it holy, even though we may be the only ones in the whole world to do so.'

"That very day we began reading the Bible and honoring God's rest day. I was about ten years of age, so it is very real to me. Mother confided to me, 'I have known about the Sabbath since about 1900, but this dream has made me change my thoughts and ways.'

"Very early one Sabbath morning a short time later,

Mother said, 'We must tell your sister Georgia that Sabbath is the day of the Lord. Let's go to her ranch today.'

"On the way I kept thinking of how Georgia might react to such sudden and unexpected news. It was at least a fifty-mile drive. As the sun rose in the early dawn I finally had the courage to try to remonstrate with Mother that she should be very tactful, so I began, 'Mother, have you ever talked with Georgia and her husband about this before?'

" 'No. That is what we are going to tell her today,' she replied, with the greatest assurance that all would be accepted as she told them.

"My attempts at suggesting caution were lost because when we got out of the car, Mother greeted Georgia by saying, 'Today is the Sabbath. We must keep it holy.'

"Unconsciously I held my breath and studied my sister's face. Her surprise was evident. But due to her deep respect for Mother, she did not protest.

"The next thing Mother said was, 'Where is your husband?'

" 'He is plowing in the field,' she replied.

" 'Go tell him to turn the horses loose, because he, too, must keep the Sabbath.'

"I anxiously waited to see what would be the reaction of my brother-in-law. My sister went down to the field, as Mother had directed, and in a short time came back with Espiridion. And do you know what he did? He turned the horses loose and came to the house. Of course, he looked bewildered, but he very politely sat with us as we all gathered around the table with our Bibles and Mother explained about the true Sabbath. And from that time onward, much to the credit of Espiridion, those horses never worked on the Sabbath again.

"Another revolutionary experience came to our family in 1940, when a man named Joe Martinez, the oldest son of Patrocino Martinez of Rancho Grande, came selling Seventh-day Adventist books. It was a two-way surprise the day Joe came to my sister's ranch. He found people keeping the Sabbath who did not know there were other Sabbath keepers in the world.

"Georgia and Espiridion learned that there are thousands of Sabbath keepers and that there is a well-organized church with missions all over the world, operated by a General Conference with headquarters in Washington, D.C.

" 'What is the name of the church?' Espiridion asked in thrilled amazement.

" 'The Seventh-day Adventist Church,' Joe proudly told them.

" 'Can we become part of it?'

This was exciting news for Joe, who assured Espiridion that Jesus' arms are always extended to include people of every race and culture.

" 'We must go to Springerville at once,' Georgia announced. 'My mother would like to hear this, because we have all kept the Sabbath for over two years. My mother, in fact, is the one who discovered this in the Bible and taught it to us.'

"It was an excited group that drove to our home that day—Joe Martinez, Georgia, and Espiridion. To add a personal touch to their already friendly contact, Joe informed the family that he had a brother also named Espiridion, a rather uncommon name.

"The group arrived at our home about four or five o'clock in the afternoon. Georgia began telling Mother the almost unbelievable news.

"Everybody brought Bibles, and we gathered around the table to listen to Joe. The night wore on, but

138

nobody thought about sleep. We gave Joe our undivided attention, read from the Bible, and asked questions. Midnight came and went. 'Why didn't we see this before?' Mother exclaimed. Finally, at one o'clock in the morning the Bible lesson ended.

"Joe told us how Jesus saved him and his family from slavery to liquor, hate, and retaliation.

"Plans were finally made for our baptism. I cannot express how happy we were to know that we were part of God's family here on earth. Georgia and Espiridion were among those baptized May 20, 1940, by Elder Homer Casebeer. Early in 1941, when I was thirteen years of age, Elder Casebeer baptized me in the lake at Rancho Grande, New Mexico.

"We attended church and camp meetings at Reserve until a few more Sabbath keepers moved into Nutrioso, which is only fifteen miles from Springerville. This gave us the inspiration to start our own Sabbath school in 1942.

"When my eldest brother, Joe, returned from the armed forces, he seemed to take pleasure in making fun of our religion. He really tried to give us all a bad time, but in the end it was he who led out in building the Springerville church.

"Mother kept active in church work as long as she lived, acting as Dorcas leader, Sabbath School secretary, also Sabbath School superintendent, and later deaconess. My father, in his zeal to share the gospel with others, would stand in the post office and hand out literature to interested people.

"The Sunday afternoon that my mother passed away, she asked us to sing as we surrounded her bed. She sang with us until her voice grew fainter; then she silently closed her eyes and went to sleep in Jesus."

After telling the preceding story, Oni, as his friends

call him, returned to Springerville and brought Joe, his brother, back to the Spanish camp meeting.

Joe had the ability of a storyteller also. This is his account of the work in Springerville: "The way we got started with the church building was that I donated the land. That started the enthusiasm. Church members from Holbrook came and helped put up the framework of the building. Then something happened and it stood that way for six years—*six years!* Nobody did any work on the church all that time. There the framework stood like a skeleton.

"One day I went up in the White Mountains to work for some millionaires. One of the woman asked what had happened to that half-built church in Springerville. People standing around looked sneeringly at me and asked, 'Oh, yes, what happened to the horse church?' They called it the horse church, because my dad had put his horses to pasture on the church land.

"Those remarks put me on the spot; so when I came back to Springerville, I called Elder Conrad Rasmussen, the minister, and said, 'Look, either you build that church or we burn it.'

" 'Why are you so angry?' he asked. 'You are not a Seventh-day Adventist Christian, are you?'

"I didn't argue with Elder Rasmussen, but asked him whether he was willing to come in every day and work on that church. He told me, 'Look, Joe, I have too many churches—Holbrook, Showlow, Chinle, Payson, and Springerville to pastor. What I will do is give you two days a week. Is that fair enough?'

"I agreed, and said, 'The days you are here, you assign the work we are to do in your absence, and I will go ahead in my spare time.

"When the church members in Reserve heard about my working on the church building in Springerville, they decided it was time for me to become a regular member in the Reserve church. But Elder Owen Jones, who was pastor by that time, said, 'No, Joe. You donated the land; you helped build the church. You are supposed to be the first one to be baptized here.' And that's the way it was. Elder Jones baptized me in 1950. Our church was dedicated April 24, 1965, free of debt. There are now thirty-five members.

"From among the children who attended our church and the church school there are now nurses, teachers, doctors, and missionaries, and I am proud to be a part of it."

A Medic's Witness

"Do you speak Spanish?" I asked a young man sitting near the back of the main pavilion between services at the Prescott camp meeting.

"Si, como no [Yes indeed]!" he smiled and replied emphatically. "My name is Nelson Harris." His smile broadened as he must have noticed the surprised look on my face. "My father was from Texas of Irish descent, and my mother, Mexican," he added quickly.

"I would like to know your life story and how you met the Lord. That is why I spoke to you," I explained.

"Very well," Mr. Harris replied, "I shall be happy to tell you of the gentle and gradual leading of the Holy Spirit in the lives of myself and of my wife.

"In 1943, at 19 years of age, I went into the armed forces. I dutifully carried the rosary with me, but thought little of God.

"I was transferred in training from one camp to another—Texas, Missouri, Pennsylvania, California, Hawaii, and finally to Okinawa. Away out there in the Pacific Ocean on that island so far from home and loved ones, I had the greatest experience of my life. It was there I really saw the power of prayer demonstrated in the life of the medic in our batallion. He was truly a faithful, genuine Seventh-day Adventist.

"In those days I gave Pfc. Arthur Opp a bad time and made fun of him until we experienced a terrible typhoon. That typhoon has gone down in American history as one of the most terrifying storms experienced by our armed forces.

"All of us soldiers ran for cover, even in the tombs, to hide when the storm arose. Some of us repeated the rosary again and again, but it gave us no security. I did not understand then that I was only praying to a dead virgin and making 'vain repetitions,' which Jesus had asked us not to do. I have since learned to talk to Him directly, just as I would to a very close friend.

"Unlike the rest of us soldiers, Pfc. Opp remained in his tent and talked to the living God, while the rest of us were running for shelter. We thought he was crazy. But when the storm had finally passed over and we ventured out of our hiding places, what a surprise awaited us. Desolation greeted us everywhere. That we expected. But to our amazement, just one lone tent was standing, that of Pfc. Opp. What an experience! What an example of faith! I will never forget that demonstration of the power of a living and loving God.

"After World War II, I returned to Quemado and my childhood sweeetheart, Sophie. We were married February 19, 1950, and since I am a lover of the great out-of-doors, I entered the United States Forest Service in Springerville, Arizona, in 1951.

"Later we were transferred to Saint Johns. It was there that our firstborn son, Stevie, drowned in an irrigation ditch near our home. The death of our little boy was the most terrible experience that had ever happened to us. I kept asking myself, 'Where is Stevie? Is he in limbo, purgatory, or heaven?' I must know.

"During our great bereavement, Onesimo

143

Gutierrez, my wife's uncle who lives in Springerville, came to give us comfort, and by his beautiful Christian hope drew me nearer to God. I had a desire to know more about God and to understand why my son had drowned, so I began to carry my Bible with me as I worked in the woods. And the Bible opened to me a vastly different idea of God than that which I had believed before.

"Another step heavenward was when my wife began reading *Golden Treasury of Bible Stories,* by A. W. Spalding.

"Soon my wife's uncle began giving us Bible studies, taking up Bible lessons by various topics. We became so thrilled with what we were hearing that we could not be satisfied. Our hunger was so great that we enrolled in a Bible correspondence course from the Voice of Prophecy. How diligently we studied, and by 1956 we were baptized into the Seventh-day Adventist church of Springerville.

"It had been the death of our son that really started us searching for a better way of life; but we see that God had been gradually leading us toward truth through one experience and then another. He has blessed our home with five children and the joyous hope of all being together with our Stevie for eternity."